HISTORIC SHIPS

THE SURVIVORS

HISTORIC SHIPS
THE SURVIVORS

Paul Brown

AMBERLEY

First published 2010

Amberley Publishing Plc
Cirencester Road, Chalford,
Stroud, Gloucestershire, GL6 8PE

www.amberley-books.com

Copyright © Paul Brown 2010

The right of Paul Brown to be identified as the Author
of this work has been asserted in accordance with the
Copyrights, Designs and Patents Act 1988.

ISBN 978 1 84868 994 7

British Library Cataloguing in Publication Data.
A catalogue record for this book is available from the
British Library.

Typeset in 10pt on 12pt Sabon.
Typesetting and Origination by FONTHILLDESIGN.
Printed in the UK.

Contents

Foreword   7

Introduction   9

1   Paddle Steamers   11
Waverley, Kingswear Castle, Compton Castle, Lincoln Castle,
Tattershall Castle, Wingfield Castle, Medway Queen, Maid of the Loch.

2   Lake Passenger Vessels   30
Gondola, Lady of the Lake, Raven, Lady Wakefield, Tern,
Swan, Teal, Sir Walter Scott.

3   Coastal and River Passenger Vessels   44
Balmoral, Manxman, Nomadic, Alaska, Coronia, Regal Lady,
Hurlingham, Karina, Kenilworth, Northern Belle, Yarmouth Belle.

4   Steam Tugs   61
Canning, Cervia, Challenge, Daniel Adamson, John H. Amos,
Kerne, Mayflower, Portwey, TID 164, TID 172, *Brent.*

5   Motor Tugs   76
Brocklebank, Calshot, Garnock, John King, Kent,
Knocker White, Severn Progress, Thomas, Wendy Ann.

6   Cargo Vessels and Tankers   87
Basuto, Cuddington, James Jackson Grundy, Safe Hand,
Advance, VIC 32, *Spartan, Vital Spark, Maggie,* VIC 56,
VIC 96, *Freshspring, Kyles, Raven, Robin, Shieldhall.*

7   Service Vessels   108
Bertha, Edmund Gardner, Explorer, John Adams, Pyronaut, Vigilant.

8   Fishing Vessels   116
Barcadale, Blue Linnet, Lydia Eva, Ross Leopard, Ross Tiger.

9   Yachts   122
Carola, Esperance, Undine.

10   Naval Vessels   126
Bronington, Iveston, Wilton, MTB 71, MTB 102, MGB 81,
HSL 102, RTTL 2757, *Western Lady IV, The Fairmile,* ML 1387,
Morning Wings, Sarinda, Vincent, MFV 74, MFV 119,
Dream Trader, Cornish Maiden, MFV 740, Old 797, *Navigator.*

Foreword by Martyn Heighton, Director, National Historic Ships

The character of Great Britain is defined by the sea. Our communities, economy, political systems, social mix, even our languages and vocabularies are the products of an island nation that developed through seaborne exploration, trade (both far-flung and close to home), conflict, and the movement of peoples from and to these islands. Today, with a shrunken mercantile navy, an empire that has faded into history, a minimal manufacturing base, and goods handled in remote automated container ports with tiny workforces, it is all too easy to forget that we are still a maritime nation. When we do think of our seagoing past, it tends to be about the harbours, docks, quaysides and warehouses through which trade passed, or the big and famous ships such as RMS *Titanic*, the Grand Fleet of the Royal Navy, and the great liners that graced the oceans up to the end of the twentieth century, all now lost to us through disaster or the passage of time.

However, our story is expressed as much in the smaller vessels that plied our coasts and rivers as it is through ships such as HMS *Victory*, SS *Great Britain*, HMS *Warrior*, *Discovery*, HMS *Belfast* or *Mary Rose*, which can be visited today and are listed on the National Register of Historic Ships. Paul Brown has taken the story of the smaller vessels, which comprise over 90 per cent of the vessels on this register and the accompanying National Archive and Overseas Watch List held by National Historic Ships, and through his book, paints a picture of the variety and richness of these survivors from a past era.

That these vessels are still with us is tribute to the passion and commitment of individuals and voluntary organisations, rather than coherent national policies. Indeed, historic ships stand out from historic buildings, quaysides, docks and landscapes by having no statutory protection. National Historic Ships is pressing for this to be changed, but when change comes, such protection will still rely on understanding and empathy for the sea and our inland waterways to make it work.

The vessels in this book cover all the activities of a thriving maritime society, from workaday ships such as tugs, cargo, fishing and service vessels, through the smaller but vital naval vessels of the twentieth century Royal Navy and exquisite, elegant steam yachts, to pleasure boats carrying thousands of passengers around our coasts and on our lakes, lochs, canals and rivers. Some have been fully restored with the vital support of the Heritage Lottery Fund, which, to date, has invested over £100 million in historic vessels. Others, particularly those in private ownership, have to make their own way. Whatever their status, you will find here vessels that are fully functioning still, despite the ravages of time and the rising difficulties and costs of meeting modern operating standards. Others are permanently berthed in harbours and docks, on inland waterways and in museums, attracting public interest as static exhibits giving fascinating insights to the past.

Whatever their use and the past technologies which they demonstrate, these vessels are tangible expressions of the lives of the people who worked on them, had fun on them, or were associated with them through the tasks and trade that they carried out. They are an integral part of our collective history and deserve to be cherished and enjoyed. This book is therefore important in telling the stories of these ships, and bringing them to life for the reader.

Martyn Heighton
Director
National Historic Ships

www.nationalhistoricships.org.uk

 National Historic Ships

National Historic Ships and its advisory committee were set up in 2006 as a non-departmental public body to advise the Department of Culture, Media & Sport, the Heritage Lottery Fund and other grant-giving organisations on priorities for ship preservation and funding. We act as a focus for advice on all aspects of the preservation of historic ships and maintain the National Register of Historic Vessels, which lists over a thousand significant craft. We support vessel owners through our small grant scheme, giving grants for repairs, preservation, conservation and training. In addition, National Historic Ships spearheads new initiatives to ensure the long-term future of traditional boat and shipbuilding skills, along with dry-docking, slipping and other shipyard facilities. We promote the interests of historic vessels within the wider heritage sector and regularly organise meetings, seminars and public forums for owners and supporters of historic vessels on matters of shared interest.

For more information, visit our website at: www.nationalhistoricships.org.uk

Introduction

The National Register of Historic Vessels lists over 1,000 craft, whilst the National Archive of Historic Vessels lists over 400 smaller craft – evidence that our maritime heritage is far from neglected despite the many problems that maintaining historic vessels presents. Included in these totals is a huge variety of craft, ranging from the few large ships that are almost household names – like *Victory*, *Cutty Sark* and *Great Britain* – to small craft of only 33 feet in length, such as the smaller yachts and canal boats. All are at least fifty years old. In this volume, a selective approach has been taken in order to focus on about 100 of the smaller powered vessels. They are mostly of over 60 feet in length, but the majority will be unknown to the general public; nevertheless, they provide valuable insights into the rich maritime history of the United Kingdom and first-hand evidence of the design and construction of small ships over a period of 125 years. Their histories as described in this book reveal the contributions they made to the commercial, leisure and naval activities of the nation during that time, and provide fascinating examples of maritime endeavour at a time when Great Britain was first and foremost a maritime nation. Featured here are passenger vessels, tugs, cargo vessels, fishing craft, service vessels, yachts and naval craft, all with a tale to tell.

One of the best ways to preserve historic ships is for them to continue in the use for which they were originally built, either commercially or as private leisure craft. For example, the tug *Wendy Ann* (which was built in 1934) is still in daily use on towing duties in the Isle of Man, and the tank barge *Safe Hand* (of 1950) continues in service on the Mersey. These are rather exceptional, but it is much more common to find historic excursion ships and ferries still plying their trade. Importantly, this latter group is also very accessible to the public, who can enjoy the experience of sailing on them on our lakes, rivers and coast. Ullswater's *Lady of the Lake* (of 1877) is believed to be the oldest working passenger vessel in the world, now under motor rather than her original steam. Some steamers are still working though, of which the best known is *Waverley*, which makes a breathtaking sight in harbours and coasts around the British Isles as she completes her ambitious excursion programme each year. *Gondola* on Coniston Water, *Kingswear Castle* on the Medway, and *Alaska* on the upper Thames are also still in steam, offering trips throughout the summer season. Many other historic motor passenger vessels provide regular trips to the public, and several vessels from other categories, including *Shieldhall*, *Mayflower* and *John King*, offer this from time to time.

A few of the ships are open to the public as floating restaurants or bars, such as *Tattershall Castle* on the Thames, *Wingfield Castle* at Hartlepool, and *Maid of the Loch* on Loch Lomond, or as museum ships, such as *Ross Tiger* at Grimsby. Others of the historic ships featured here are less accessible: in most cases, they can at least be viewed from the dockside, but not boarded, though several are berthed in commercial dock systems where the public cannot usually gain easy entry.

When viewing the ships, it is not uncommon to find that they are in poor condition, their owners or custodians overwhelmed by the costs involved in maintaining and preserving them. The Heritage Lottery Fund sometimes comes to the rescue, but one fears that some of the ships are suffering a long and lingering death. It is always refreshing to know of the major rebuilds that return the ships to pristine condition: the coaster *Robin* and drifter *Lydia Eva* are recent examples. Private owners of smaller craft sometimes achieve near miracles of restoration, and the vessel becomes a 'live-aboard' for them. One solution – available in rare cases only – is almost to start again, building a completely new hull and fitting as much of the original fixtures and equipment as possible. This happened to *Gondola* (which is virtually a replica) and is in progress with *Medway Queen* (where more of the original ship will survive).

The information in this book has been retrieved from many places, but the register entries on the National Historic Ships website have provided the starting point in most cases. I am grateful to Hannah Cunliffe, of National Historic Ships, and to many of the owners of the vessels featured for their help in sourcing photographs and additional information, and to other photographers who have generously provided images, their names being credited in the relevant places. Websites dedicated to many of the ships featured have provided much useful information. Some details of coastal forces service histories have been sourced from the British Military Powerboat Trust. Others who have provided information include Richard Basey (*MTB 102* Trust), Steven Carter, Christian Grammer, David Kampfner, Andy King, Philip King, Martin Stevens, Chris Monkhouse, Philip Simons, and Steve Richardson. Special thanks go to Andrea, who accompanied me on some of the ship visits and made many valuable suggestions.

I hope that you, the reader, will find that this book stimulates your interest in these ships and I encourage you to visit and, where possible, sail on them.

CHAPTER 1

Paddle Steamers

WAVERLEY

The London & North Eastern Railway (LNER) ordered a new paddle steamer in 1945 to replace war losses (in particular, the *Waverley* of 1899 had been sunk at Dunkirk in 1940). The new ship, also named *Waverley*, was built for service on the Clyde by A. & J. Inglis at Pointhouse, Glasgow, the keel being laid on 27 December 1945. With shortages of materials, there were some delays to construction, but the launch took place on 2 October 1946, and the ship was berthed in the River Kelvin for fitting out. Trials took place in June 1947, and *Waverley* moved to her base at Craigendoran for her maiden voyage on 16 June.

Designed on pre-war paddle steamer lines, *Waverley* was one of the last traditional paddle steamers to be built. Of imposing appearance, she had a raked stem, cruiser stern, two masts, and two large, raked funnels. She was painted in the traditional LNER colours – her funnels with a black top, white stripe and red bottom, the traditional fan-slotted and decorated black paddle-boxes, black hull with two gold lines, red boot topping and white waterline, cream upperworks, brown deck shelters and silver railings. Her original colour scheme lasted only one season, for in 1948, the railways were nationalised and the railway steamers' ownership passed to the British Transport Commission (BTC). *Waverley*'s funnels were repainted in the buff (pale yellow) with black top colours of the Caledonian Steam Packet Co. (CSP), the division of BTC that operated the Scottish steamers. She was coal-fired, though she was converted to burn oil in the winter of 1956/57. In 1959, her paddle-boxes were painted white. Her splendid 66-inch-stroke triple-expansion engines could be viewed by the passengers on the main deck between the lounge and the restaurant. On the promenade deck were two deck shelters, the forward one for first class passengers and the after one for third class passengers: this two-class accommodation was the norm on railway company vessels.

Waverley's main excursion route in the early days was the cruise from Rothesay to Loch Goil and Loch Long, known as the Three Lochs Tour, since most passengers left the ship at Arrochar, at the head of Loch Long, to journey over to Tarbet for a sail on Loch Lomond, rejoining *Waverley* at Craigendoran. Before the cruise, she operated the 8.45 a.m. ferry run from Craigendoran to Dunoon and Rothesay and, at the end of the day, returned with a ferry service from Rothesay to Craigendoran,

Left: *Waverley*'s funnels, photographed in 2004. (Keith Belfield)

Below: A postcard view of *Waverley*, date stamped 3 August 1956, showing the British Transport Commission livery with buff-coloured funnels, adopted after the nationalisation of the railways. The message on the reverse reads, 'We are spending the day on Loch Lomond, where this ship brought us … all you need is a mac and some good wellingtons, for everything is beautiful except the rain.'

Waverley alongside the pier at Yarmouth, Isle of Wight, in September 2004, during her annual visit to the Solent area. (Keith Belfield)

In 1979, for the second year running, *Waverley* spent the early part of her season on the South Coast and Thames. Here she steams out of Newhaven Harbour in April 1979, one year after her first visit to the port. (Author)

and her crew, who had been working since 6 a.m., did not finish until about 8.30 p.m. *Waverley*'s weekend duties took her into Loch Fyne and the Kyles of Bute. On 7 October 1947, she finished her season and was laid up for the winter in Bowling Harbour.

For twenty-seven seasons, she continued to operate in the Firth of Clyde and the adjoining lochs, both on excursions and regular ferry services. Winters were not always spent in lay up – between 1949 and 1954, she had a variety of winter duties, often replacing another ship that was being overhauled, or she was the spare vessel lying in dock with steam up ready to cover for other vessels in an emergency. In the main season, her routes were extended to include the Isle of Arran in 1953, visiting Brodick and Whiting Bay. From 1958 onwards, there was also a cruise up the Clyde to Glasgow (Bridge Wharf) from the coastal resorts, allowing holidaymakers to view the shipbuilding and merchant shipping on the river. In 1965, like other railway vessels, her hull was repainted in monastral blue, and red metal lions rampant were emblazoned on the funnels. In 1969, Caledonian Steam Packet became part of the Scottish Transport Group, no longer under railway control, and in the following year, the hull was painted black again. By 1970, she was the last seagoing paddle steamer in the world.

By 1971, *Waverley* was one of only two large excursion vessels left on the Clyde and, for the first time, was based at Gourock. (The other vessel was the turbine steamer *Queen Mary II*, which was withdrawn in 1977 and became a restaurant and function venue on the Thames, but is now in France.) In 1972, the paddle-boxes were repainted black. In 1973, CSP became part of Caledonian MacBrayne Ltd. *Waverley*'s funnels had another makeover, becoming red with a yellow circle encompassing the lions. The continued decline in traffic meant that 1973 was to be *Waverley*'s last season.

On 8 August 1974, she was sold for a nominal £1 to the Paddle Steamer Preservation Society, thus saving her from the ship-breakers. Rather than becoming a static exhibit, she was refitted for the *Waverley* Steam Navigation Company, a limited company formed by the enthusiasts who had saved her, and her livery was returned to the smart LNER colour scheme of red, white and black. In 1975, she re-entered service on the Clyde, sailing at weekends from Glasgow (Anderston Quay) and in mid-week from Ayr. In 1977, *Waverley* spent a week on excursions from Liverpool, the first time she had ventured beyond the Firth of Clyde, and the success of this led to over a month being spent on the South Coast in the following year. In 1981, she was fitted with a new boiler and embarked on her first full season of Round Britain cruising, with the peak summer weeks spent back on the Clyde. This has extended her season considerably and has helped make her operation viable. In her winter 1990/91 refit, the paddle wheels were replaced, and a major £3 million two-stage rebuild was undertaken in early 2000 and winter 2002/03 by George Prior at Great Yarmouth, with the support of the National Heritage Lottery Fund. Her decks and deckhouses were removed and central and aft portions of the hull were completely stripped and the engines dismantled and rebuilt. A new boiler was installed and the deckhouses were repainted in scumbled wood-effect finish in conformance with the original LNER scheme. In the second stage of the rebuild, her forward accommodation was rebuilt and the forward deck shelter and foremast replaced.

She continues to be maintained in excellent condition and is the last seagoing paddle steamer in Europe. Fully restored and painted in her original London & North Eastern Railway colours, *Waverley* makes an exciting sight under steam as, to the sound of the rapid beat of her paddles, she approaches and leaves the many harbours and piers that are included in her crowded itinerary.

Her season typically starts on the Clyde at Easter, followed by sailings out of Oban during the early May Bank Holiday weekend. She remains in the Clyde and west of Scotland area until early June, when she moves to the Bristol Channel for two weeks. *Waverley* returns to the Clyde at the end of June and stays until the end of August. Much of September is spent on the South Coast between Weymouth and Worthing, before moving to the Thames area (between Dover and Great Yarmouth) towards the end of the month and continuing until mid-October, when she returns to the Clyde for a final few sailings.

Gross registered tonnage: 693. Length: 239.6 feet (73.03 m). Beam: 30.2 feet (9.2 m). Draught: 6.5 feet (1.98 m).
Propulsion: Triple-expansion diagonal steam engine, oil-fired, 2,100 ihp. Speed: 14 knots (cruising), 18.4 knots (maximum on original trials).
Passengers: 1,350.

KINGSWEAR CASTLE AND COMPTON CASTLE

The picturesque River Dart was the cruising ground of three small excursion paddle steamers until the 1960s. One of these vessels, *Kingswear Castle*, has been fully restored to steaming condition and is based at Chatham Historic Dockyard in Kent. She was built on the Dart by Philip & Son of Dartmouth in 1924 as a practically identical sister to *Compton Castle* of 1914 (which survives as a hulk at Truro) and *Totnes Castle* (1923). Her coal-fired engine, built by Cox & Co., Falmouth, was transferred from an earlier *Kingswear Castle* and, like that ship, dated from 1904. *Kingswear Castle* was completed with an enclosed wheelhouse and was later fitted with flying bridges that doubled as landing bridges to improve boarding facilities at low water. There was also a slightly raised coach deck running along the centre of the afterdeck above the after saloon. The fore saloon was equipped with a small catering bar.

The trio, owned by the River Dart Steamboat Co., carried holidaymakers from Dartmouth, or Kingswear, to Totnes during the summer season. During the Second World War, *Kingswear Castle* was initially used by the Admiralty as a stores depot at Dittisham. In 1941, she was chartered by the United States Navy as a liberty ship, carrying personnel and stores at Dartmouth, still in her peacetime livery. She returned to her peacetime duties in 1945, and in the winter of 1961/62, a new boiler was fitted.

A postcard photo of *Kingswear Castle* at the Landing Stage, Totnes, during her time in service on the Dart.

The restored steam engine in *Kingswear Castle*. (Chris Allen)

She became the last paddle steamer on the Dart and the 1965 season was to be her last, at the end of which she was laid up in Old Mill Creek.

In the spring of 1967, she was bought by the Paddle Steamer Preservation Society (PSPS) for £600 and in August of that year was towed to the River Medina, Isle of Wight, for charter to Riddetts in whose marina *Medway Queen* was in use as a clubhouse and restaurant and was occasionally in steam in the Solent. This charter was intended to be a stopgap until the society raised enough funds for conservation of the ship. However, in the spring of 1970, *Kingswear Castle* was moved from her river mooring to a mud berth and became subject to vandalism and her condition deteriorated. PSPS terminated the charter, and in June 1971, she was towed to the Medway. A restoration project gathered momentum, and by November 1983, she was able to steam again on trials. For the 1984 season, she did not have a full DTI certificate and could only take twelve passengers on her sailings from Strood Pier. After further work, a certificate for 250 passengers was issued in May 1985 and she started a programme of sailings from the Thunderbolt Pier, in Chatham Historic Dockyard. A plan to return the ship to the River Dart was dropped, and *Kingswear Castle* has remained in service carrying passengers on afternoon, evening and charter cruises on the Medway and Thames. Further renovation has since involved replacing all the decks and the underwater steelwork, and in spring 2001, she received a new coal-fired boiler, built by Wellman Robey of Oldbury, near Birmingham, to a traditional design similar to its predecessor.

Her season runs from April until October (but not every day, except during the main summer school holidays), and most cruises start from either Chatham Historic Dockyard or Rochester Pier. Occasional sailings are made from Whitstable or Southend, and group charters are also offered. Some special all-day cruises are offered, for example, on the day of the Medway sailing barge race. The on-board facilities include two saloons below deck with a café/bar in the forward saloon. Half of the upper deck is covered with an awning with roll-down canvas side screens for use in bad weather.

Gross registered tonnage: 94. Length: 113.7 feet (34.7 m). Beam: 17.5 feet (5.3 m) – hull, 28 feet (8.5 m) – overall. Draught: 3 feet (0.9 m). Paddle wheel diameter: 10 feet (3 m).
Propulsion: two-cylinder compound diagonal reciprocating steam engine. Single Scotch boiler. Speed: 8 knots. Bunkers: 4 tons coal.
Passengers: 235. Crew: 5.

Kingswear Castle's near-sister ship *Compton Castle* was built by Cox & Co., Falmouth, (who later built the engines for *Kingswear Castle*) and completed in 1914 for the River Dart Steamboat Co. She was the first Dart steamer to have wide, extended decks over the elongated sponsons and an elevated deck over the aft well deck, and had an open navigating platform, which was enclosed as a wheelhouse in the 1920s. In the Second World War, she was requisitioned as a naval ammunition

The hulk of *Compton Castle*, in use as a coffee shop and florists at Lemon Quay, Truro, January 2005. (Chris Jones)

carrier on the River Dart. Her peacetime sailings on the Dart resumed in 1947 and continued until 1962. At the end of the 1962 season, the Board of Trade surveyor decided that the boiler would need to come out for inspection and might have required renewal as well as very extensive re-plating of the hull. The owners decided to retire her and removed the wheelhouse, rails, companionways, teak doors, lifebuoys and boat, which were all fitted to a new motor vessel.

Compton Castle was sold in 1964 to Bourne & Woods and became a floating museum and tearoom at Squares Quay, Kingsbridge. A new wheelhouse and rails were fitted and her hull was repainted white. In July 1964, she was towed from Dartmouth to Kingsbridge. Her forward saloon housed a café and her aft saloon a small museum. Visitors were able to view the engines, which were kept in working order, and in 1966, she steamed under her own power for the last time, for the filming of a television commercial. In 1978, Salcombe Harbour Authority ordered the removal of the vessel after the owners failed to provide Board of Trade certification that her hull was sound. She was sold to Ernest Clayton and taken to Looe, Cornwall, for a planned restoration to working order. However, this project failed, and in 1982, she was sold again to David Worlledge to become a restaurant ship at Lemon Quay, Truro. Her engines were removed and sold to the Bembridge Museum, Isle of Wight; they are now on display at the Blackgang Chine Museum. A large deckhouse was constructed, which largely destroyed her original appearance. In 1990, she became a florists and coffee shop and continued in this role until 2008 when, by now in poor condition, she was sold to restaurateur Kevin Viner, who plans to refit her as a nautically themed restaurant and tearoom.

Gross tonnage: 97. Length: 108 feet (32.9 m). Beam: 28 feet (8.5 m). Draught: 3 feet (0.9 m).
Propulsion: two two-cylinder compound diagonal reciprocating steam engines driving paddle wheels.
Speed: 8 knots.

WINGFIELD CASTLE, TATTERSHALL CASTLE AND LINCOLN CASTLE

For forty years, three paddle steamers plied between Hull and New Holland on the ferry service across the River Humber, until about 1974, when they were replaced by a diesel-electric paddle car ferry (which was, in turn, made obsolete by the opening of the Humber Bridge). All three of the paddle steamers have survived: *Wingfield Castle* at the Museum of Hartlepool, *Lincoln Castle* as a bar and restaurant ship at Grimsby, and *Tattershall Castle* as a floating pub and restaurant on the Thames Embankment, close to Hungerford Bridge.

Wingfield Castle was built by W. Gray & Co. Ltd, Hartlepool, for the London and North Eastern Railway. Her keel was laid on 27 June 1934, and she was launched three months later on 24 September by the lady mayoress of Hull; on the same day, her sister ship *Tattershall Castle* was also launched from the same yard. Their engines were manufactured by Central Marine Engines Works, Hartlepool.

Wingfield Castle in Sealink colours during her service as a ferry between Hull and New Holland, on the Humber. (Martin Stevens)

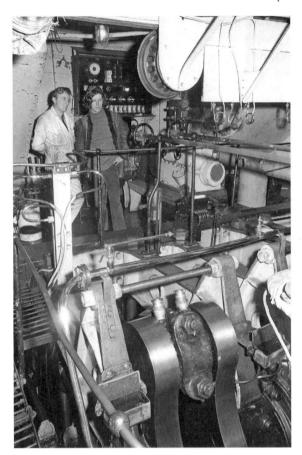

Left: The engine-room in *Wingfield Castle* during her Sealink days. (Martin Stevens)

Below: *Wingfield Castle* in 2007 at the Museum of Hartlepool, where she is berthed on the former shipyard site of her builders, William Gray & Co. (Author)

Tattershall Castle seen in 2009 as a pub and restaurant ship on the Thames Embankment. (Author)

An early view of *Tattershall Castle* in service on the Humber. (Campbell McCutcheon)

Tattershall Castle in British Railways colours. (Campbell McCutcheon)

The third, and later, vessel of the class, *Lincoln Castle*, was Clyde-built by A. & J. Inglis, Pointhouse, and was launched on 27 April 1940. She differed from the two earlier ships in having her boiler forward of the engine, and the funnel was therefore further forward. Her maiden voyage to Grimsby from the Clyde was routed around the north of Scotland and into the North Sea, because the war made a Channel passage too risky. She was damaged in a storm and had to return to the Clyde for repairs; she eventually completed the voyage successfully at the second attempt in spring 1941.

On the ferry service between Hull and New Holland, they mainly carried passengers, but the large open main deck aft could also carry a small number of cars, and pens for livestock. During the twenty-minute crossing, first class passengers could use the forward saloon and deck, where a snack bar was provided. Third class passengers were restricted to the rear of the ship, including a cramped 'lounge' largely below water level beneath the open deck aft. *Wingfield Castle* carried a lot of livestock, and on one occasion, a cow fell down the companionway into the crew's quarters and proved rather difficult to remove. On another occasion, a frightened cow fell overboard in mid-river, but blithely turned around and swam back to the shore. The steamers also provided Sunday excursions to Read's Island and Grimsby until 1967. During the Second World War, *Wingfield Castle* ferried troops and supplies along the Humber. In 1948, when the railways were nationalised, ownership of the three steamers passed to the British Transport Commission, and then, in 1963, to the British Railways Board, and later Sealink. Finally, *Wingfield Castle* made her last ferry crossing on 14 May 1974 and was withdrawn from service.

Lincoln Castle seen in Sealink colours during her service as a Humber ferry. (Martin Stevens)

Wingfield Castle was bought by the Brighton Marina Company but her conversion costs proved prohibitive and she was sold. After being laid up in the King George V Dock, London, she was sold to Whitbread for use as a floating pub at Swansea, but this scheme also fell through – because she was too wide to pass through the dock gates at Swansea. She remained at Swansea for four years before being purchased by Hartlepool Council in June 1986 and was then taken to her birthplace at Hartlepool for restoration, which was carried out between 1987 and 1992. She became a floating restaurant and conference centre and was opened to the public as a museum exhibit by the Museum of Hartlepool. By 2007, she was in need of further restoration and a £800,000 refit was undertaken. Visitors can tour the ship at the Hartlepool Maritime Experience (where HMS *Trincomalee* is also berthed) and use the coffee shop on board. Her berth is on the former site of William Gray & Co., her builders.

Tattershall Castle was used briefly during the Second World War as a tethering vessel for barrage balloons in the Humber estuary before returning to duty ferrying troops and munitions, and she was one of the first civilian vessels to be equipped with radar. Her postwar service on the Humber ferry continued until 1973 when she was laid up. In 1976, she was sold to become a floating art centre and conference centre on the Thames. In 1981, she was sold to the Chef & Brewer Group, and repairs and a refit were carried out by Acorn Ship Repairs on the River Medway. She reopened as a pub and restaurant ship on London's Victoria Embankment in 1982. A further refit was carried out by Crescent Marine Services on the Medway in 1991, and another costing £4.75 million in 2003-04 by George Prior at Great Yarmouth. Her appearance progressively changed to incorporate an enclosed main deck aft, a new bridge structure with large windows replacing the wheelhouse. Larger windows were cut into the forward lounge on the port side, and the paddle wheels were removed (and the ship lost her distinctive fan-shaped paddle-box vents). She is thus much more substantially altered than her two sister ships. Her original engines are still in place and can be viewed behind glass by visitors. She is now owned by the Spirit Group, who bought the retail business of Scottish & Newcastle Breweries in 2003, and remains a very popular venue.

Lincoln Castle remained in service until 1976, when she was the last coal-fired paddle steamer operating in British waters. She was sold in 1979 to Francis Daly of Hull and, in 1981, became a floating pub at Hessle close to the Humber Bridge, under the ownership of PS *Lincoln Castle* Ltd. She was subsequently re-sold to Colin Johnson and moved to Immingham in 1987 for refurbishment. In 1989, she opened as a restaurant and bar at Grimsby and is now berthed at the National Fishing Heritage Centre there. She has been closed to the public since 2006 'for maintenance', though her future seems uncertain.

Gross tonnage: 556 (Lincoln Castle 598). Length: 209.5 feet (63.9 m). Beam (including paddle-boxes): 56 feet (17.1 m). Beam (hull): 33 feet (10.06 m). Draught: 4.5 feet (1.37 m).
Propulsion: Triple-expansion, diagonal-stroke, reciprocating steam engine (coal-fired), 1,500 ihp. Speed: 12 knots.
Passengers: 1,050. Car capacity: 20.

MEDWAY QUEEN

In the heyday of the paddle steamer, families could escape from the industrial towns and cities and, filling their lungs with sea air, be transported to the piers of nearby seaside resorts. This era is epitomised by *Medway Queen*, which sailed from the Medway towns to Southend, Margate, Herne Bay and Clacton and survives as the last estuary paddle steamer. After years of decay, she is undergoing a remarkable transformation, in which her engines and fittings are being installed in a new hull.

Built for the New Medway Steam Packet Co. Ltd by Ailsa Shipyard, Troon, (who also built her engines) she was launched on 23 April 1924. Her design was based on the Ailsa-built *Bournemouth Queen* of 1908, with a near full-length promenade deck, traditional paddle-boxes, single tall funnel, pole mast and an open flying bridge: there was no wheelhouse and the captain and helmsman were protected only by white canvas dodgers.

After trials on the Clyde, she sailed to Rochester to replace the company's *Princess of Wales* and join their other paddler, *City of Rochester*, operating from Strood and Sun Pier, Chatham. The New Medway Steam Packet Company had

A postcard view of *Medway Queen* on her sea trials in 1924.

A postwar postcard view of *Medway Queen* arriving at Southend Pier after crossing from the Kent coast on an excursion.

The restored funnel and paddle-boxes of *Medway Queen*, on display ashore at Chatham Historic Dockyard in 2009. They will be returned to the restored ship's new hull during fitting out at Bristol. (Author)

been formed in 1919 with the assets of the Medway Steam Packet Company, which dated from 1837, having first been formed to operate a ferry service between Chatham and Sheerness before the arrival of the railway. In 1936, the New Medway company was taken over by the General Steam Navigation Company (GSN), which operated paddlers on the Thames in addition to its fleet of short sea cargo and passenger ships: this gave GSN a monopoly of the Thames excursion trade. Nevertheless, the New Medway company kept its own name, identity, and livery of black hull, white promenade deck sides and cream funnel emblazoned with the company badge. *Medway Queen* was present at the Coronation Review of the Fleet at Spithead in 1937.

In 1938, she was converted from coal to oil-fired steaming by the Wallsend Slipway & Engineering Company. In 1939, she carried children who were evacuated from Kent to East Anglia, before being requisitioned by the Admiralty on 9 September for war service as a minesweeper. Her conversion to that role was carried out at the GSN yard in Deptford Creek. A 12-pounder gun was fitted on the forecastle and a Hotchkiss gun was mounted on each paddle-box. Minesweeping gear was fitted aft and an enclosed bridge cabin was constructed. Repainted grey, she hoisted the White Ensign as HMS *Medway Queen* and displayed the pennant number J48. At first, she was based at Harwich and carried out daily sweeps of the Thames and Medway estuaries. She was then transferred to Dover to join the 10th Minesweeping Flotilla patrolling the Dover Straits.

On 28 May 1940, *Medway Queen* was anchored off the South Coast, spotting enemy aircraft laying mines, when she was ordered to proceed to Dunkirk to assist in the evacuation of the British Expeditionary Force from the beaches and was one of the first ships to arrive on the scene. Her motorised dinghy was used to ferry the troops out. As the ship returned to Dover with her first load of troops, she was attacked by German fighter planes and her machine-guns downed one of them. She came upon the sinking paddler *Brighton Belle*, which had hit a submerged wreck, and rescued many of her survivors. On the following day, *Medway Queen* entered Dunkirk harbour amid heavy gunfire. The oil tanks were ablaze by then and there was wreckage everywhere. Another full load of troops was embarked and the ship returned to Ramsgate. In all, she made seven trips between 27 May and 3 June and rescued about 7,000 men. The ship's galley was kept busy giving every soldier a plate of stew and a mug of cocoa during the return crossings.

That she played a leading and heroic part at Dunkirk is illustrated by the fact that she made more trips across the Channel than any ship other than destroyers. Seven awards for gallantry were gained by her crew and three enemy aircraft were shot down. On the last trip, the starboard paddle-box was badly damaged by a destroyer that had hauled up alongside after being hit by shells, but *Medway Queen* managed to limp back to Dover Harbour and had to be repaired at Chatham Dockyard. For her part in this massive operation, which saw 338,266 men lifted in 848 craft of all types, she was awarded the battle honour 'Dunkirk (Operation *Dynamo*) 1940'.

In about 1943, *Medway Queen* became a minesweeping training ship until being returned by the Admiralty to her owners in January 1946. A refit by Thornycroft at Southampton followed and she returned to the excursion trade in 1947. Her regular itinerary started at Strood, with calls at Chatham (until 1959) and Sheerness (until 1954), and onward to Southend and either Clacton or Herne Bay. In June 1953, she was present at the Coronation Review of the Fleet at Spithead. After seventeen postwar seasons, she made her last sailing on 8 September 1963.

In January 1964, she was towed to the East India Dock, London, and initial preservation attempts were made. In the event, she was sold to Alan and Colin Riddetts to become a marina clubhouse on the River Medina, Isle of Wight, was towed there in January 1965 and opened in her new role on 14 May 1966. She was also in use as a nightclub but was replaced by the paddle steamer *Ryde* and became derelict. In 1984, she was sold and moved back to the Medway on a pontoon and berthed at St Mary's Wharf, Chatham. This was the start of a very protracted and fraught process to secure her survival and restoration, and shortly afterwards, the *Medway Queen* Preservation Society was formed. The ship sank at her moorings before being towed, on 1 November 1987, to Damhead Creek, Kingsnorth, on the Hoo Peninsula.

Eventually, a solution to restore the ship to full working condition was arrived at. The hull had deteriorated beyond repair, so the ship was dismantled to salvage the engines, paddles, and other equipment, the funnel, paddle-boxes and some decking. All this was to be reconditioned and installed in a new hull, the latter being funded through a £1.86 million grant from the Heritage Lottery Fund, which was announced in June 2006. The dismantling was completed in October 2006 and plans were made for construction of the hull by A. & P. Tyne. However, this proposal was rejected by the Heritage Lottery Fund on the advice of the National Historic Ships Committee because the hull was to be welded rather than riveted. Eventually, an order for a riveted hull was placed with David Abel (Shipbuilders) of Bristol on 3 October 2008. The engines were transported by road from Chatham Dockyard to Bristol's Albion Dry Dock (where the hull was to be constructed) on 6 December 2008. The first steel of what was to be the first fully riveted ship to be built in England for over fifty years was laid in the Albion Dry Dock on 6 June 2009. It is not expected that the completed ship will obtain a passenger certificate. Instead, she will be mainly used alongside as a hospitality and museum ship, at a berth somewhere on the Medway, with the possibility of being steamed for occasional trips with a skeleton crew.

Gross tonnage: 316. Length: 180 feet (54.9 m). Beam: 24 feet (7.3 m). Draft: 5.5 feet (1.7 m).
Propulsion: Paddles driven by compound diagonal reciprocating steam engine; Scotch boiler with triple furnaces.
Speed: 13 knots at 45 rpm cruising, 15 knots at 55 rpm maximum speed.

MAID OF THE LOCH – PADDLE STEAMER

The last major paddle steamer to be built in the UK, *Maid of the Loch* sailed on Loch Lomond from 1953 until 1981 and later became a static restaurant and exhibition ship there. Ordered in 1950 by the British Transport Commission from A. & J. Inglis of Pointhouse, Glasgow, she was built and then cut into sections for transportation by rail to Balloch on Loch Lomond. There she was re-assembled and was launched, almost complete, without ceremony, on 5 March 1953. Her two-cylinder compound diagonal engine was built by Rankin & Blackmore of Greenock. The ship had a full-length promenade deck and further open deck space on the upper deck. Her accommodation included two observation lounges, two bars, a cafeteria, and a seventy-seat restaurant forward on the main deck. Between the main and promenade decks, she had four curved stairways housed within the paddle sponsons. Much use was made of aluminium in the superstructure and funnel to help reduce her draught. She was painted white overall with green boot-topping, a buff funnel, and had the British Railways lion and wheel crest on her bows. In the 1975 season, her funnel colour was red with a black top. Her mainmast was removed in 1978.

A service had first been initiated on Loch Lomond in 1818, and it is believed that this was the first regular passenger steamer service on an inland lake anywhere in the world. *Maid of the Loch* was the twentieth paddle steamer to have sailed on Loch Lomond. She ran trials on 4 May 1953 and was named at a

Maid of the Loch in service on Loch Lomond during the 1970s. (Andrew Lindsay)

ceremony on 22 May, prior to a special cruise to Ardlui. The maiden cruise with fare-paying passengers took place on 25 May. Her regular route took her from Balloch to Ardlui with calls in either direction at Balmaha, Rowardennan, Tarbet and Inversnaid. From 1964, *Maid of the Loch* terminated at Inversnaid following the closure of the pier at Ardlui, though cruises to the Head of the Lake were also operated. During each winter, she was laid up. The Caledonian Steam Packet Company took over the ship in 1957, followed in 1969 by the Scottish Transport Group, and in 1970 by William Alexander & Sons – when the British Railways emblem was removed. Her last season was 1981 after which she was laid up at Balloch pier and her condition deteriorated badly.

In 1992, *Maid of the Loch* was acquired by Dumbarton District Council and efforts to save the ship began with volunteer working parties; at the end of 1995, she was transferred to the *Maid of the Loch* Trust prior to the establishment of the Loch Lomond Steamship Company, a registered charity. In 1997, her wooden deck was replaced with steel. Her lower hull was painted black, with red boot-topping, above which the main deck sides and the superstructure remained white, but the funnel was now red with a black top. Grants obtained in 2000 enabled a restaurant, bar/café and exhibition area to be created on board. Following the restoration of the steam-powered slipway at Balloch, she was hauled out of the water in June 2006 (for inspection) for the first time since her withdrawal, as part of her rebuild – the objective of which is to return her to service.

Gross registered tonnage: 555. Length: 193 feet (58.83 m). Beam: 28.1 feet (8.56 m); 51 feet (15.54 m) including paddle-boxes. Draught: 7.1 feet (2.16 m).
Propulsion: Two-cylinder compound diagonal steam engine, 900 ihp; oil-fired boiler.
Speed: 13.75 knots (trials), 12 knots (service).
Passengers: 1,000.

CHAPTER 2
Lake Passenger Vessels

GONDOLA

The steam yacht *Gondola* that sails on Coniston Water in Cumbria is to all intents and purposes a replica of the original vessel that was built in 1859 for the Coniston Railway Company. Only a small number of fittings from the original vessel were incorporated into the 'restored' *Gondola*, which was completed in 1980. However, this should not be allowed to detract from the pleasure of taking a trip on this authentic steam-powered yacht as she makes her smooth and near-silent progress on Coniston Water in the beautiful surroundings of the adjacent fells. She is the only steam-powered vessel offering a regular passenger service in the Lake District.

The original vessel was ordered for the Coniston Railway Company, which had opened a line in 1859 to carry ore from the mineral workings around Coniston to Barrow-in-Furness. One of the company's directors, Sir James Ramsden, saw the opportunity to transport tourists to the Lake District with the highlight of a cruise on one of the lakes. The design of *Gondola* is thought to be based on the Venetian *Burchiello*, which Ramsden may have seen on a Grand Tour of Europe. Her hull of wrought-iron plates on steel frames was built in four sections by Jones & Quiggin, Liverpool, and transported by train and cart to the a slipway near Coniston Hall, where the vessel was assembled before being launched in December 1859. *Gondola*'s two-cylinder steam engine and boiler were built by Lawrence & Co. of Liverpool. She had first and third class cabins, reflecting her railway company ownership.

Gondola entered service on Coniston Water in 1860. Two years later, the company was acquired by the Furness Railway Company. Many of the passengers lived in industrial Lancashire and holidayed on the Fylde coast. Following the purchase by the railway company of four paddle steamers between 1900 and 1908 trippers could be brought from Fleetwood to Barrow. There they took a train to Greenodd and a horse-drawn coach from Greenodd to Lake Bank, on Coniston Water, where they boarded *Gondola* for a trip to Waterhead, and returned by train from Coniston to Barrow. The more adventurous tourists could even extend their trip by taking a horse-drawn excursion from Coniston to Ambleside. *Gondola* carried around 20,000 passengers each year during this period.

Gondola stops briefly at Monk Coniston Pier at the northern end of Coniston Water to embark and disembark passengers in April 2009. (Author)

Gondola leaves Monk Coniston Pier to continue on her loop to Coniston and Brantwood. (Author)

Gondola maintained regular sailings until the First World War, when she was laid up. After the war, she was recommissioned, and in 1923, the copper locomotive-type boiler, which supplied steam at 80 psi, was replaced by a vertical steel boiler giving 100 psi. In the same year, following the railways regrouping, she was taken over by the London, Midland & Scottish Railway and continued in service until being withdrawn in 1936. Her engine and boiler were then removed to power a local sawmill.

In 1946, *Gondola* was sold to Fred McCaddam of Barrow, and became a houseboat at Water Park, near the southern tip of Coniston Water. In 1963, a storm tore her from her moorings and drove her onto the shore where she became derelict and half-sunk. In the mid-seventies, local staff members of the National Trust took an interest in her, and in January 1977, holes in the hull were filled with cement and the hull was raised and moved to near Coniston Hall. In 1978, she was acquired by the National Trust, which commissioned a survey, revealing that the hull was beyond repair. The construction of a new welded steel hull and new superstructure was initiated when the keel was laid in September 1978, the work being carried out by Vickers Shipbuilding & Engineering Ltd at Barrow-in-Furness as an engineering project for their apprentices. The old hull was cut into four sections and taken to Barrow, where the lines were taken off.

The old wrought-iron gunwhale plate (the curved edge of the vessel, where the deck meets the hull) was saved, as were some of the barley-twist wrought-iron handrails and railings, and were incorporated into the new *Gondola*. The new hull was transported in four sections to Coniston on 3 September 1979 to be assembled and fitted out. A new steam engine, built by Locomotion Enterprises, of Gateshead, and a boiler by Bertram Brothers, also of Gateshead, were installed. The new horizontal steel boiler supplies steam at 150 psi and is based on the design of a Ffestiniog Railway locomotive boiler. At first painted green, it was repainted for the 2009 season in the maroon of the Furness Railway with the company's crest emblazoned upon it, in anticipation of the original vessel's 150th anniversary in 2010.

The new *Gondola*'s elegant lines, ornate bow decorations with carvings of the coat of arms of the Duke of Devonshire (the 7th Duke was the chairman of the Furness Railway) dominated by a gilded sea serpent, and plush, red-patterned-velvet-upholstered first class saloon with decorated walnut details combined to recreate the splendour of her Victorian appearance. The upholstery of the third class saloon is covered in red leather. The large plate glass windows in both saloons afford splendid views for passengers even when they are seated.

On 25 March 1980, she was launched by Sheila Howell, great-granddaughter of Felix Hamill – who was master of *Gondola* for fifty years. The new vessel entered service again on 24 June 1980, 120 years after being first commissioned. Since then, she has operated daily sailings during the season (1 April to 31 October), carrying up to eighty-six passengers from Coniston Pier. In all, about 34,000 passengers are now carried each year. Latterly, the open navigating platform has had a glass wheelhouse added. From March 2008, *Gondola* has burned sustainable logs made from wood waste, instead of coal.

In 2009, her normal forty-five-minute route took in calls at Brantwood and Monk Coniston and a loop towards the southern end of the lake, turning off Torver Common (no longer calling at Park-a-Moor as she had earlier done). Twice weekly, a longer, ninety-minute cruise explored the full length of Coniston Water. *Gondola* is also available for private charters and wedding receptions.

Gross tonnage: 42. Length: 84 feet. (25.62 m). Beam: 15 feet. (4.57 m). Draught: 4.6 feet. (1.4 m).
Propulsion: Locomotive-type boiler supplying two-cylinder (V-twin) steam reciprocating engine, 14 hp, single screw. Speed: 11.7 knots maximum, 8 knots cruising.
Passengers: 86. Crew: 3.

TERN

The first passenger steamer on Windermere (or indeed any English lake) was the paddle-driven *Lady of the Lake*, of 1845, which was owned by the Windermere Steam Yacht Co. A rival company, the Windermere Iron Steamboat Co., was formed in 1847, and eleven years later, the two companies merged as the Windermere United Yacht Co. The Furness Railway bought shares in the company in 1866 and, in 1872, took sole control. By then, there were rail lines from Ulverston to Newby Bridge and from Kendal to Windermere, opening up the Lake District as a tourist destination for the masses for the first time and generating traffic for the increasing number of lake steamers.

Tern approaching Bowness from Lakeside in April 2009. Refitted to resemble a steamer, she has an enclosed wheelhouse positioned well forward and an awning over the top deck. (Author)

A postcard view of *Tern* as a steamer in the 1950s on Windermere. Her open navigating platform is just forward of the funnel.

In 1890, the Furness Railway ordered a new vessel from Forrest & Co., of Wivenhoe in Essex. She was to have been named *Swallow*, but after a last-minute change, she was launched in June 1891 as *Tern*, a coal-fired twin-screw steamer with a passenger capacity of 633. Transported in sections by rail from Wivenhoe to Windermere, she was assembled at Lakeside, and when she entered service, she was the largest steamer on the lake. Her two sets of twin-cylinder steam engines were manufactured by Westray Copeland of Barrow-in-Furness and produced 200 hp. A distinctive feature of her appearance, which has been retained to this day, was the canoe bow. She had two masts, and an open navigating platform just forward of her tall, thin funnel, which was positioned amidships.

In November 1893, she sank at her Lakeside moorings in severe gales but was refloated the same night. In 1923, the railway regrouping took her into the ownership of the London, Midland & Scottish Railway. During the Second World War, she was moored at Bowness Pier as sea cadet training ship, with the unit taking the name TS *Undine* after a submarine that had been built at Barrow. In 1948, railway nationalisation led to *Tern*'s ownership passing to the British Transport Commission, whose fleet later became Sealink. In the winter of 1957/58, *Tern* was re-engined with two six-cylinder 120-bhp Gleniffer diesels, her tall funnel was replaced by a squat, raked funnel, and she was reclassified as a one-class ship. An enclosed wheelhouse was later erected over the navigating platform.

In 1984, Sealink was privatised and the new owners were Sea Containers Ltd, who renamed the Windermere operation 'The Windermere Iron Steamboat Company'. In 1993, the fleet returned to private, local ownership when the Bowness Bay Boating Company purchased it, and it now operates as Windermere Lake Cruises.

In the winter of 1990/91, *Tern* was refitted to more closely resemble her original steamer appearance: a tall, thin funnel was reinstated, an enclosed wooden wheelhouse was erected at the forward end of the upper deck, and an awning was constructed to cover the remaining part of the upper deck. She now presents an elegant, Victorian steamer profile, albeit with the practical expedient of retaining her diesel engines. The fore and aft saloons are attractively furnished with patterned, green, velvet upholstery and dark woodwork and the after saloon has a café/bar. She operates on the Lakeside/ Bowness/Waterhead (Ambleside) route, typically making three round trips in the day during the main season.

Gross tonnage: 120. Length: 145.7 feet (44.4 m). Beam: 18 feet (5.5 m). Draught: 9 feet (2.75 m).
Propulsion: twin-screw Cummins diesels (installed in 1997-98).

SWAN AND *TEAL*

These two motor vessels were built in the 1930s for the London, Midland & Scottish Railway as part of a plan to update and improve their Windermere cruise fleet. First off the stocks was *Teal*, which was built by Vickers Armstrong at Barrow-in-Furness in 1936. She was transported in sections by rail, reassembled

A postcard date stamped July 1957 shows *Swan* in a close-to-original configuration. She has no funnels, an open navigating platform and top deck, and the main deck saloon has open gangways running down each side.

An empty *Teal* approaches Bowness in April 2009 prior to the first trip of the day, showing her latest appearance. (Author)

at Lakeside, and launched on 4 July 1936. Her first passenger certificate was for 877 people on three decks in first and third class accommodation. At this time, she had an open top deck and open bridge, and the main deck saloon had open gangways running down each side of the main structure. There were no funnels – instead the engine exhausts were led through the lower side of the hull, well aft.

Her sister ship, *Swan*, followed in 1938. Again, she was built at Barrow by Vickers Armstrong, and was launched at Lakeside on 10 June 1938. She was identical to *Teal* except that a slight modification to the design meant she did not need to carry ballast. Both ships operated a limited service in the early years of the Second World War, until the end of the 1941 season, when they were laid up for the duration of the war. The service resumed on 16 July 1945. In 1948, ownership passed to the British Transport Commission and subsequently Sealink. In August 1956, Queen Elizabeth II and Prince Philip sailed on *Teal* from Ambleside to Bowness.

Both ships had first and third class accommodation. *Teal*'s first class observation saloon was furnished with wicker armchairs. The brochure for *Swan*'s inaugural passenger sailing stated that her 'first class accommodation is luxurious and comprises open decks, observation lounge and tea saloon. For third class passengers, there is also a splendid upper deck and commodious lounge and tea saloon'.

Over the years, the two ships have been modernised several times and they became single class. The bridge has been enclosed, the main deck saloons have been extended to the full width of the hull, and the top deck has received successively more permanent canopies. In 1994, twin funnels were constructed abreast at the after end of the top deck. Thus their appearance combines elements of the old and new, not always entirely satisfactorily – the new funnels seem particularly incongruous. *Teal*'s original 160-bhp Gleniffer diesel engines were replaced by new Kelvin diesels in 1993, whilst *Swan*'s Gleniffers were replaced by new Cummins diesels in 1996. Both vessels later had bow thrusters fitted.

Like *Tern*, *Teal* and *Swan* are now operated by Windermere Lake Cruises who maintain a year-round service on the Lakeside/Bowness/Waterhead route, on every day except Christmas Day. The timetable is co-ordinated to connect with the Lakeside and Haverthwaite Steam Railway at the southern end of the lake.

Gross tonnage: 251. Length: 141.9 feet (43.25 m). Beam: 25 feet (7.62 m). Draught: 9.3 feet (2.83 m).
Propulsion: twin-screw Kelvin diesels (Cummins in Swan*).*
Passengers: 560.

LADY OF THE LAKE

Lady of the Lake is believed to be the oldest working passenger vessel in the world. She was launched on 26 June 1877 by T. B. Seath & Co., of Rutherglen, Glasgow, for the Ullswater Steam Navigation Company. The latter company had been formed

An early picture of *Lady of the Lake* as a steamer, approaching the Ullswater Hotel Pier, probably taken before 1900. She has an open navigating platform abaft the funnel. (Ullswater 'Steamers')

This view of *Lady of the Lake* off Silver Point shows her still in steam, but with an enclosed wheelhouse forward of the funnel, replacing the open navigating platform. (Ullswater 'Steamers')

in 1855 to transport mail, passengers, provisions, and slate and lead from nearby mines, between Patterdale and Pooley Bridge on Ullswater, Cumbria. In 1900, the company became the Ullswater Navigation & Transit Company, and around this time, the original pier at the Ullswater Hotel (now the Inn on the Lake) in Patterdale was moved to the current location (now known as Glenridding), just nearby.

Lady of the Lake's iron hull was transported in three sections by rail to Penrith and then by horse-drawn drays to Waterside, where she was constructed at Elder Beck and completed on 12 July 1877. Her original certificate of registry describes her as having one mast, rounded stern, iron framework, clencher fastened.

In November 1881, *Lady of the Lake* sank at her moorings and was refloated by a team of Liverpool divers. From 1910, she was a Royal Mail steamer, carrying mails from Howtown to Patterdale. In 1936, her steam engine was replaced by Kelvin diesels, providing 115 bhp: these were later replaced by Cummins diesels. In 1958, she sank again, in a gale at Pooley Bridge, and was refloated with the help of the local fire brigade. In 1965, *Lady of the Lake* was badly damaged by fire whilst on the Glenridding slipway and remained out of service until being completely rebuilt, and was re-launched on 19 May 1979.

She is painted in the company livery – a pale-green hull with white upperworks, and a red funnel with black top. Her small saloon is rather utilitarian in its furnishings, and has a small café/bar. With the company's other vessels, she maintains a year-round passenger service from Glenridding to Pooley Bridge, via Howtown, on every day except 24 and 25 December. The company now operates as Ullswater 'Steamers'.

Gross tonnage: 42.7. Length: 97 feet (29.57 m). Beam: 14.75 feet (4.5 m). Draught: 2.4 feet (0.73 m).
Propulsion: twin Cummins diesels, 180 bhp, two screws. Speed: 9 knots (cruising).
Passengers: 247. Crew: 3.

RAVEN

Raven joined *Lady of the Lake* on Ullswater in 1889, replacing the troublesome paddle steamer *Enterprise*, which had been the first of the Ullswater Steam Navigation Company's craft. Like *Lady of the Lake*, *Raven* was built by T. B. Seath at Rutherglen and was transported in sections to Ullswater, where she was launched on 11 July 1889. The *Cumberland & Westmoreland Herald* described the new vessel, saying, 'It is questionable if there be any boat to beat, or even equal this little craft on any lake in this country.' *Raven* was named after Ravencragg, the home of one of the company's directors.

In 1912, *Raven* was made a temporary royal yacht and her decks were painted yellow to mark the visit of the German Kaiser, Wilhelm II, to Lowther Castle. In

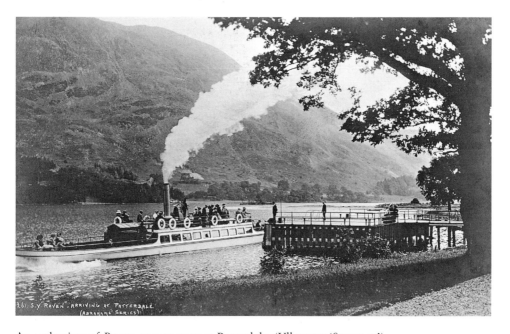

An early view of *Raven* as a steamer at Patterdale. (Ullswater 'Steamers')

Raven on Ullswater in April 2009. (Author)

1934, she was converted from steam and was fitted with National Gas diesels, and subsequently, in 1965-66, with twin Thornycroft AEC diesels, cruising at about 10 knots. These have since been replaced by Cummins diesels.

She has a larger saloon than *Lady of the Lake*, with a larger café/bar area, but also of rather utilitarian design.

Gross tonnage: 62.7. Length: 112 feet (34.1 m). Beam: 15 feet (4.57 m). Draught: 2.85 feet (0.87 m).
Propulsion: twin Cummins diesels, 155 bhp, two screws. Speed: 9 knots (cruising).
Passengers: 220. Crew: 3.

LADY WAKEFIELD

In 2007, *Lady Wakefield* joined the Ullswater 'Steamers' fleet to allow continuous winter sailings to be maintained and to accommodate daytime charters by groups and coach parties during the peak season. This motor vessel had spent the first fifty-six years of her life as an excursion boat in south Devon, having been built in 1949 by Philip & Son, Dartmouth, as *Berry Castle*, for the River Dart Steamboat Company Ltd. She was a steel-hulled vessel with space for 150 passengers and cruised on the River Dart between Dartmouth and Totnes. In 1972, she was sold and renamed *Golden Cormorant*, operating at Fareham and Rochester. In 1977, she returned to the Dart as *Totnes Castle*, and was now owned by Dart Pleasure Craft. Under the latter name, she was sold to Plymouth Boat Cruises in 1985 and ran a summer ferry service from Plymouth to Cawsand and occasional trips to Looe.

Lady Wakefield at Patterdale in April 2009. (Author)

In July 2005, she was sold to Ullswater 'Steamers', who wished to acquire a 'heritage' vessel in keeping with the others in their fleet. After a delivery voyage to Whitehaven, the vessel was transported to Ullswater by road; because of height restrictions, the superstructure had to be removed for this journey. A two-year refurbishment on a slipway near Pooley Bridge was finished in March 2007, and she was recommissioned in a ceremony by HRH Princess Alexandra at Glenridding Pier on 17 April 2007. The total cost of the project to the company was around £550,000, well in excess of that originally envisaged, due to the amount of new plating found to be necessary on the hull. The vessel has improved facilities, including wheelchair access. The name *Lady Wakefield* honours the wife of Lord Wakefield, who acquired the Ullswater Navigation & Transit Company in 1953.

Gross tonnage: 58. Length: 67 feet (20.4 m). Beam: 16 feet (4.9 m). Draught: 3.6 feet (1.1 m).
Propulsion: twin Gardiner 6LXB diesel engines, two screws. Speed: 8 knots (cruising).
Passengers: 150. Crew: 3.

Sir Walter Scott seen some time before 1955, with square saloon windows. (Campbell McCutcheon)

Sir Walter Scott seen in February 2010, showing the new deckhouse on the foredeck. (George Lanyon)

SIR WALTER SCOTT

Since 1900, the steamer *Sir Walter Scott* has graced the inland waters of Loch Katrine and still has her original triple-expansion steam engine. She was ordered from Matthew Paul, Dumbarton, who built the engine and sub-contracted construction of the hull to William Denny Bros Ltd, also of Dumbarton. The hull was transported in sections by barge up Loch Lomond, and then dragged by horse-drawn cart up the steep hill from Inversnaid and overland to Stronachlachar on Loch Katrine, where she was reassembled and launched in 1899. Her first owners were Robert Blair of Hotel Trossachs, Perthshire, and Donald Ferguson of the Stronachlachar Hotel, Stirling, (the latter was later bought out by the Duke of Montrose) who formed the Loch Katrine Steamboat Co.

In 1902, the wheel, which had been on deck level forward of the funnel, was raised on a platform to give the helmsman better visibility, and a bridge was later added. In the late 1940s, a wheelhouse was added. In December 1952, ownership passed to the Water Department, City of Glasgow Corporation (Loch Katrine being a source of drinking water for Glasgow). This was the first of a number of water authorities to own the ship after successive reorganisations of local authorities and water boards. She was re-boilered in 1955, and the square saloon windows were replaced by portholes, which enhanced her appearance. In 1969, her owners became the Lower Clyde Water Board and her yellow funnel was repainted white. In 1997, she was re-boilered, and ownership transferred to West of Scotland Water. From 2002, she was operated by Scottish Water.

In 2005, The Steamship *Sir Walter Scott* Trust, was formed to own, operate and preserve her. With the help of the Heritage Lottery Fund, a major conservation and restoration programme was embarked upon, which was staged over several years and involved replacement of about 85 per cent of the steelwork in the hull. In the winter of 2006/07, a bow thruster was fitted. Until the end of the 2007 season, she was coal-fired, but the overhaul included the complete renovation of the engine and the installation of two new boilers to run on biofuel from the start of the 2008 season. In the winter of 2008/09, the superstructure was rebuilt to include an unsightly enclosed lounge on the foredeck, which has spoiled the appearance of the ship.

Sir Walter Scott's usual timetable provides a return trip from Trossachs pier to Stronachlachar in the mornings and shorter cruises, which do not land, in the afternoon. Her season lasts from Easter until the end of October and around 75,000 passengers are carried each year.

Gross registered tonnage: 115. Length: 110 feet (33.5 m.). Beam: 19 feet (5.8 m.). Draught: 5 feet (1.5 m.).
Propulsion: three-cylinder triple-expansion steam engine, 140 ihp, single screw.
Complement: 5.

CHAPTER 3

Coastal and River Passenger Vessels

BALMORAL

By the 1930s, motor vessels were beginning to replace paddle steamers on coastal ferry and excursion work. After the Second World War, when building programmes resumed, they became the norm. The cumbersomely named Southampton, Isle of Wight & South of England Royal Mail Steam Packet Company, known more informally as the Red Funnel Line, needed to replace two paddle steamers lost in the war and, in October 1947, ordered the motor vessel *Balmoral* from John I. Thornycroft & Co. Ltd, of Woolston, Southampton. Her design was based on the company's pre-war *Vecta*, with changes that included reversing the locations of the semi-enclosed car deck and the dining saloon, so that the latter was forward instead of aft. Her raked red funnel had a horizontal black top and she had two masts – the mainmast was a stub mast but was later increased to full height. The promenade deck had two saloons, though these restricted deck space.

Balmoral, whose engines were also built by Thornycroft, was launched on 27 June 1949 and started trials at the end of October, attaining a speed of 16.25 knots, although her service speed was 14 knots. She entered year-round service on the Southampton – Cowes route in December 1949 and, from 1952 onwards, was also used for summer excursion work from Southampton. Her car deck became an impromptu sun deck on these occasions. One popular excursion was the Round the Island cruise, also picking up passengers at Southsea. These excursions and a range of charters took her further afield on the South Coast from Brighton to Swanage. She was also used as a tender to ocean liners lying in Cowes Roads, ferrying passengers to Southampton. On one such occasion, in November 1961, she collided with the Italian liner *Fairsky*, and *Balmoral*'s starboard lifeboat was smashed and she sustained a gash in the side of the hull – fortunately, no passengers were on board. The summer season of 1968 was her last with Red Funnel and she was offered for sale, having been replaced by a dedicated car ferry.

In the event, she was chartered to P. & A. Campbell Ltd, Bristol, to replace a paddle steamer, and was eventually purchased by them in 1978. From May 1969 onwards, she was employed in excursion work in the Bristol Channel area, adopting the white funnel livery of the Campbell fleet. Cruises to and from the resorts of Ilfracombe, Weston and Minehead were complemented by passenger-

Right: Balmoral at Southampton in her Red Funnel days. (Campbell McCutcheon)

Below: Balmoral in June 2005 approaching Portsmouth to collect passengers for a cruise around the international fleet assembled at Spithead. (Author)

Balmoral entering Portsmouth Harbour in June 2005 when she was offering cruises around the Trafalgar 200 Fleet Review at Spithead. (Author)

ferry work to Lundy, and there was an annual four-day cruise to the Scilly Isles, calling at Penzance and St Ives. *Balmoral* occasionally went to Padstow and Tenby, and sometimes charters took her back to the South Coast in the Weymouth and Solent areas, and to North Wales, Liverpool and the Isle of Man. She was later based at Swansea, until being withdrawn at the end of the 1979 season. In 1980, she was chartered by White Funnel Steamers, a company set up with the support of the Landmark Trust, which owned Lundy, to continue the island service, but made her last sailing on 14 October 1980.

Balmoral was sold to become a floating pub and restaurant at Dundee in 1982, but this venture failed. The Paddle Steamer Preservation Society purchased her in March 1985 for continued work as a cruise vessel, operated by Waverley Excursions and complementing *Waverley*. A refit equipped her with a new dining saloon aft, where the car deck had been. She spends the main summer season cruising in the Bristol Channel, typically offering sailings from Swansea, Penarth, Porthcawl, Newport, Clevedon, Weston, Minehead and Ilfracombe, and also taking in trips to Lundy Island. In June and early July, she operates in North Wales and the north-west of England (e.g., from Garlieston, Whitehaven, Portaferry and Menai Bridge), the South Coast (West Bay, Southampton, Portsmouth, Eastbourne and Rye), and the Thames Estuary and East Coast (Ramsgate, Margate, Southend, Gravesend, Tower Pier, Ipswich and Great Yarmouth). On 27 June 2009, exactly sixty years after her launch, the ship celebrated her Diamond Jubilee with a cruise from Southampton around the Isle of Wight, with calls at Cowes and Portsmouth.

Gross registered tonnage: 688 (later 736). Length: 203.5 feet (62.03 m). Beam: 32 feet (9.75 m). Draught: 8.9 feet (2.71 m).
Propulsion: two six-cylinder Newbury Sirron diesels, 1,200 bhp (replaced in winter 2002/03 by Grenaa diesels), twin screws. Speed: 14 knots.
Passengers: 750.

EGREMONT

Now lying in the Salcombe estuary in Devon, the Mersey ferry *Egremont* was launched by Philip & Son at nearby Dartmouth on 12 December 1951 for the Wallesey Corporation, which operated ferry services across the Mersey to Liverpool from Seacombe and New Brighton. Named after a suburb of Wallesey, the ship reached a top speed of 13.38 knots on trials and left the Dart for Liverpool on 31 March 1952.

Like her sister ship, *Leasowe*, her forward saloon extended to the whole width of the ship and housed a bar area and dance floor, making her suitable for cruising as well as the regular ferry services. Unfortunately, this arrangement had the drawback that there was only one gangway, the lack of a forward gangway meaning that embarkation and disembarkation of passengers could not be simultaneous. Nevertheless, she could make up to 100 crossings between Seacombe and Liverpool in twenty-four hours, and thirty-four trips between Liverpool and New Brighton in a fourteen-hour period. On 1 December 1969, the Wallesey ferry fleet merged with the Woodside (Birkenhead) fleet under the

Egremont underway. (Campbell McCutcheon)

Egremont as a floating accommodation and headquarters ship for the Island Cruising Club in the Salcombe Estuary. (Island Cruising Club)

newly formed Mersey Passenger Transport Executive. The white and black funnel of *Egremont*'s original livery was repainted in primrose yellow and powder blue, and later became emerald green and black. In 1971, the ferry service from New Brighton was withdrawn. *Egremont* continued in service until 1975 and was then laid up in Morpeth dock for a year whilst a buyer was sought. During this time, she sprang a leak, which damaged her engines and other equipment, rendering her inoperable. She was sold to Frederick Oldhand Ltd, who stripped out her machinery and sold her on to the Island Cruising Club (ICC), Salcombe.

Egremont arrived at Salcombe on 17 June 1976 to become the floating headquarters and accommodation ship for ICC, which offered sailing training and adventure holidays. Club members converted her, with an additional timber deckhouse on the boat deck aft; she can now sleep ninety people, including staff, and approximately 1,000 people pass through her each season. Opening for her first season in 1977, her hull was painted dark green, with white upperworks and a yellow funnel with black top. Latterly, she has had a black hull with a yellow band, and a white funnel, resembling her historic colours. She is dry-docked every five or six years for maintenance.

Gross tonnage: 566. Length: 145 feet (44.12 m). Beam: 34 feet (10.36 m). Draught: 12.25 feet (3.73 m).
Propulsion: Crossley diesels (since removed). Speed: 13 knots.
Passengers (originally): 700.

MANXMAN

Manxman is a classic coastal turbine steamer, now the last of that type remaining in the United Kingdom, but her future is bleak following a failed restoration project, and she may soon be scrapped. For twenty-seven years this Mersey-built Irish Sea ferry operated the service between Liverpool and the Isle of Man at a time when there was a thriving trade taking holidaymakers to the island for traditional seaside holidays. She was ordered on 24 March 1953 from Cammell Laird Ltd, Birkenhead, as the last of a class of six similar vessels, and launched on 8 February 1955. Her engines were manufactured by her builders, whilst the boilers were by Babcock and Wilcox.

On trials, she made 21.95 knots on the Firth of Clyde and was handed over to the Isle of Man Steam Packet Co. on 14 May 1955. On 20 May, she sailed light to Douglas, Isle of Man, before making her maiden voyage to Liverpool on the following day. She operated a year-round service (and summer excursions) until 1966, after which – following the introduction of car ferries – part of each winter was spent in lay-up at Birkenhead. In 1967, her original two-class accommodation was converted to single class. As more car ferries entered service, *Manxman*'s sister ships were progressively withdrawn, and by 1981, she had become the

Manxman in the covered dry dock at Sunderland, showing the white and blue livery adopted during her time as a restaurant and nightclub ship. (Ron Eyres)

last of her class in service. 1982 was to be her last season, and she made her last sailings, from Liverpool to Douglas and back, on 4 September.

She was sold on 21 September 1982 to Marda (Squash) Ltd to become a floating museum and visitor centre in a new leisure complex at Preston, to where she sailed on 3 October. She was not a success in this role and was converted into a successful floating restaurant and nightclub, remaining in Preston until 1990, when she was displaced by redevelopment of Preston Docks. In November 1990, she was towed to Liverpool to become a floating nightclub in the Trafalgar Docks, opening in 1991. This was not viable and she closed for business at the end of 1993. By this time, her black hull and red and black funnel had been replaced by a white and blue livery. *Manxman* was towed to Hull to be berthed in a disused dry dock. Parts of the ship were vandalised over the next few years, and a fire, which broke out in August 1997, seriously damaged many of the original wood panels in the former ladies third class lounge. In September 1997, the ship was towed to the yard of Pallion Engineering Co. Ltd, Sunderland, where she remains. In July 1999, she sank at her moorings but was salvaged and is now in a covered dry dock.

In May 2002, the *Manxman* Steamship Co. was formed to try to secure the future of the ship. A conditional offer of a suitable berth was obtained from the Mersey Docks & Harbour Board (MDHB) and a planned restoration project (contingent on Heritage Lottery funding) was to be filmed by Channel 4. However, MDHB was taken over by Peel Holdings and the offer of a berth was withdrawn. As a result, the project is being wound up.

Gross tonnage: 2,495. Length: 344 feet (104.85 m). Beam: 47 feet (14.33 m). Draught: 12 feet (3.66 m).
Propulsion: two Pametrada steam turbines, 8,500 shp. Speed: 21 knots. Range: 1,000 nm.
Passengers: 1,049 first class plus 1,344 third class (2,032 single class from 1967). Crew: 60.

NOMADIC

On 15 July 2006, the SS *Nomadic* returned to Belfast, where she was built by Harland & Wolff for the White Star Line, after an absence of just over ninety-five years. For many of those years, she had served at Cherbourg as a tender, taking passengers to and from the great White Star and Cunard liners when they called there on their transatlantic voyages. Now the *Nomadic* Trust hopes to restore the vessel for display in Belfast, with visitors being attracted by her associations with the *Titanic*.

Nomadic was one of two tenders ordered by the White Star Line to serve their mammoth new liners, *Olympic* and *Titanic*, at Cherbourg – where they anchored in the harbour because they were too large to berth in the port. *Nomadic* was fitted out in a luxurious style, for she would carry first and second class passengers

Nomadic at Cherbourg. (White Star Momentos)

Nomadic alongside RMS *Queen Mary*. (White Star Momentos)

Nomadic on her return to Belfast, before restoration. (White Star Momentos)

from the passenger terminal to the liners. The other tender, *Traffic*, carried third class steerage passengers. *Nomadic* was laid down on 22 December 1910 and was launched from Harland & Wolff's No. 1 slip on 25 April 1911. Nearby, on No. 3 slip, loomed the massive structure of *Titanic*. *Nomadic*, whose engines were also built by Harland & Wolff, was handed over to White Star on 27 May 1911: four days later, *Titanic* was launched and *Olympic* was handed over to her owners.

Nomadic left Belfast Lough together with *Olympic* (which was bound for Southampton via Liverpool), and arrived at Cherbourg on 3 June 1911. She tendered *Olympic* for the first time on 14 June, when the liner called for passengers on her maiden voyage to New York. On 10 April 1912, *Nomadic* sailed out from the port with 274 passengers to meet *Titanic* on her first, and only, crossing. On 25 April 1917, *Nomadic* was requisitioned by the French government and went to Brest to serve as a troopship for the US 7th Infantry Division for almost two years. After the First World War, she returned to Cherbourg and met the Cunarder *Caronia* on the first postwar transatlantic calling in Cherbourg on 2 September 1919. In 1934, White Star Line merged with Cunard and *Nomadic* was sold to the Société Cherbourgeoise de Remorquage and renamed *Ingenieur Minard* after the engineer who created the modern harbour of Cherbourg. At this time, the new harbour became operational and liners could be berthed in the harbour, largely making the tenders redundant. In June 1940, *Nomadic* sailed to Portsmouth to be requisitioned by the British government as a troopship. With the war in Europe over, she returned on 8 July 1945 to Cherbourg, where she was again in demand as a tender because war damage had rendered the port inaccessible to large liners. For a further twenty-three years, she performed this work, ending when she serviced *Queen Elizabeth* for the last time on 4 November 1968.

She was sold for use as a floating restaurant and function venue in Paris. Her engines, funnel, several internal bulkheads, and superstructure were removed during the conversion, and she did not arrive in Paris until October 1974. She opened to the public on 26 June 1977 and gave twenty-two years service in this role. By 1999, new regulations required that she be dry-docked regularly for inspections, but her location made this infeasible, and her owners went into administration. She was seized by the Paris harbour authorities in 2002 and moved to Le Havre in April of the following year. In January 2006, *Nomadic* was sold at an auction to Northern Ireland's Department for Social Development for £170,000 and brought back to Belfast on a submersible barge. At the time of writing, she is still owned by the department and a conservation plan is being prepared prior to tenders going out for her restoration, subject to funds being available.

Gross tonnage: 1,273. Length: 233 feet (71.02 m). Beam: 37 feet (11.28 m). Draught: 7 feet (2.13 m).
Propulsion: two compound steam engines. Speed: 12 knots.
Passengers: approx. 1,000.

Alaska steaming on the upper Thames. (Ian Boyle)

ALASKA

Now the oldest working steamer on the Thames, *Alaska* was built in 1883 by J. S. & W. J. Horsham & Co., Bourne End, for W. H. Barebrook of Walton-on-Thames. In 1887, she was sold to Salter Bros, Oxford, to inaugurate their weekly return service between Oxford and Kingston in the following year. The passage to Kingston took two days, and the return trip three days, with passengers staying overnight in hotels and guest houses. In later years, she was used as a private party boat at Oxford. In the Second World War, she served in the Thames River Patrol. In August 1943, she was sold to Jackson Bros Ltd, Putney, for further service before being bought by Mears of Twickenham for trips between Richmond and Teddington.

Alaska was later sold to Putney Sea Scouts, who took out the steam plant and used her as their headquarters. Around 1948, she was sold to R. Horton, as a hulk, and was used as a hire boat pontoon at Medley Boat Station in Oxford. In 1974, she was rediscovered there and became a restoration project. Her original engine (which was built by Seeking of Gloucester) was located and restored, and with a new boiler and restored hull, she steamed again in July 1987. Since 2006, she has been owned and operated by her skipper, Peter Green, under the auspices of Thames Steamers, and is normally engaged in charter work between April and November, based in Marlow, Buckinghamshire. On bank holiday weekends and during the Henley Regatta, she sometimes offers public trips from Bourne End Marina.

*Gross tonnage: 16. Length: 60 feet (18.3 m). Beam: 9.5 feet (2.9 m). Draught:
3.2 feet (0.98 m).*
Propulsion: two-cylinder steam engine (fired with high-density wood briquettes).
Passengers: 36.

CORONIA

Coronia is one of two historic excursion vessels running trips from Scarborough.
She was built as *Brit* by Fellows & Co., Great Yarmouth, in 1935 for Longfield
Brothers, who offered excursions from Great Yarmouth's Town Hall Quay and
Britannia Quay. She was licensed to carry 200 passengers and spent her first five
summers taking holidaymakers out to see the seals basking on the sandbanks
along the North Sea coast of Norfolk. She was powered by twin Crossley diesels.
Following the outbreak of war, she was requisitioned by the Admiralty on 16
September 1939 for service as a tender. Renamed *Watchful*, she carried stores and
torpedoes to destroyers anchored in Yarmouth Roads. On 29 May 1940, she was
deployed to assist in the Dunkirk evacuation and reportedly rescued 900 troops.
On 12 December 1945, she was returned to her owners and was refitted and
restored to her original name for the start of the 1946 season. In 1950, *Brit* was

Coronia at Scarborough. (National Historic Ships)

modified with a lower funnel and bridge to be operated on the Thames by Thames Launches for excursion work during the Festival of Britain.

In spring 1951, she was sold to D. Dalton & G. Round for excursion work at Scarborough and renamed *Yorkshire Lady*. She was repainted with a white hull and a yellow funnel, which later had the company's house flag emblazoned on it. In 1954, the company became Scarborough Cruises Ltd. In a 1961 refit at Eyemouth, *Brit* was re-engined with Gardner 6LX diesels, increasing her speed from 10 to 12 knots, and a new wheelhouse was fitted. In 1968, she was sold to J. W. Johnson and renamed *Coronia*. Her service in the Scarborough excursion trade continued, and in 1980, ownership passed to Don Robinson. Then, in 1985, she was sold to Tommy Hanson and sailed for Gibraltar, where she offered excursions to view the Rock and marine life around the colony. In 1991, *Coronia* was sold to North Sea Leisure (owned by Tom Machin) and, on 5 June of that year, returned to Scarborough, where she resumed service alongside *Regal Lady*. She continues to make coastal cruises from there and occasional trips to Bridlington. In 2007, her bottom was extensively re-plated.

Gross tonnage: 75. Length: 88 feet (26.82 m). Beam: 19.5 feet (5.94 m). Draught: 5 feet (1.5 m).
Propulsion: twin Gardner diesel engines.

REGAL LADY

Regal Lady was built as *Oulton Belle* by Fellows & Co., Great Yarmouth, in 1930 for the Yarmouth & Gorleston Steamboat Co. and operated excursions out of Great Yarmouth and Lowestoft. She was a double-ended steamer, with a propeller at each end, capable of 10 knots. She took part in the Dunkirk evacuation in late May/early June 1940, and then returned to Great Yarmouth. Subsequently, she was requisitioned and based at Greenock for duties as a tender to troopships on the Clyde. *Oulton Belle* was returned to her owners on 17 December 1945 and resumed work between Yarmouth and Gorleston together with trips on the Norfolk Broads. In the winter of 1948, she was taken in hand at Fellows' Southtown shipyard and her bow propeller was removed, an upper deck was installed, and the old funnel was replaced by a modern one (but she remained a steamship). Her route was changed to a sea trip to Lowestoft, returning to Great Yarmouth via the Broads and Beydon Water.

On 23 May 1954, *Oulton Belle* was sold to Scarborough Cruises Ltd and renamed *Regal Lady*. She arrived at Scarborough in the following month and embarked on her first season as an excursion vessel there. Her steam engine proved unsuitable for the new work, and during the winter of 1954/55, it was removed, cut up and placed in the ship's bottom as ballast (where it remains). A 160-bhp, eight-cylinder Gleniffer diesel engine was fitted, giving a cruising speed of 10 knots. *Regal Lady* continued in service at Scarborough until the end of the 1970 season, when she was

Stern view of *Regal Lady* at Scarborough. (National Historic Ships)

sold to Neville Blake, of Chedgrave near Norwich, who operated her on river trips from Norwich for the next fourteen years. Her last sailing was on 30 September 1984, after which she was laid for two years. She was then sold to Tom Machin (owner of North Sea Leisure) for further service at Scarborough, where she arrived on 8 January 1987 after a twenty-two-hour passage. *Regal Lady* was then rebuilt with a new GRP wheelhouse and her steel superstructure was extended. On 24 May 1987, she re-entered service at Scarborough after a break of seventeen years, and continues to operate there with *Coronia*.

Gross tonnage: 72. Length: 74 feet (22.56 m). Beam: 16.5 feet (5 m). Draught: 7 feet (2.1 m).
Propulsion: Gardner diesel engine.

HURLINGHAM

This Thames excursion launch was built in 1915 as a tunnel-stern steamship by Salter Brothers Ltd for Joseph Mears, of Richmond, and could carry up to 325 passengers. The tunnel stern was developed to protect the propeller from weeds and other debris. Her compound steam engine was built by W. Sisson. She was involved as one of the

Hurlingham seen on the Thames in 2009. (Author)

'little ships' in the Dunkirk evacuation in May 1940. For most of the Second World War, she was part of the River Emergency Service as a supply tender. In 1947, she was acquired by Thames Launches and was converted to diesel power. In 1978, she was sold to Marine Transit Ltd, and from 1979, was operated by Tidal Cruises Ltd (later Thames Cruises). She has been gradually upgraded and modernised, with enclosed accommodation. Between 1983 and 2002, *Hurlingham* ran from Westminster to Greenwich and since then has been used for charters. In the early hours of 20 August 1989, she was on passage near Southwark Bridge when her crew and passengers witnessed the collision between the dredger *Bowbelle* and another Thames Cruises' excursion launch, *Marchioness*, which sank. *Hurlingham* rescued over twenty survivors from the water, whilst fifty-one people lost their lives.

Gross tonnage: 114. Length: 101.2 feet (30.85 m). Beam: 16.6 feet (5.06 m). Draught: 4 feet (1.22 m).
Propulsion: Leyland Thornycroft diesel engine.

KARINA

This former Devon ferry and excursion vessel is now in commercial service at Douglas, Isle of Man. She was launched on 17 June 1946 by Philip & Sons Ltd, Dartmouth, at their Noss Shipyard as *May Queen* for the Oreston & Turnchapel Steamboat Co., Plymouth, and was the last passenger ferry to be built for that company. She was constructed of carvel planking on oak frames, her design having its origins in the company's steam ferries of the 1880s. Her maiden voyage was on 27 July 1946 and she worked for eleven years as a Plymouth ferry before being sold in 1957 to the rival firm, Millbrook Steamboat & Trading Co. Ltd, who refurbished her and renamed her *Eastern Belle*. She worked on the Tamar estuary, with ownership passing to Dart Pleasure Craft in 1980, and thereafter, she also made occasional trips from Dartmouth. In 1985, Dart Pleasure Craft pulled out of Plymouth services, and she was sold to Plymouth Boat Cruises Ltd, who operated her until 1988. She was sold again to G. H. Ridalls & Sons Ltd, of Dartmouth, and was renamed *Totnes Princess* in March 1989. She ran from Dartmouth to Totnes and also made trips out to sea as far as Torquay and Hallsands. She remained in service on the Dart until 1999, when Ridalls sold their fleet to Dart Pleasure Craft, who had by then been purchased by Dart Valley Railway Plc. *Totnes Princess* was surplus to the new company's requirements, and in September 2001, she was sold to Laxey Towing Company of Douglas, Isle of Man, (owners of the tug *Wendy Ann*, q.v.) for coastal service. They renamed her *Karina* after a famous Manx excursion vessel of 1913. She is currently licensed to carry 100 passengers and offers cruises from Douglas and private charters.

Gross tonnage: 20. Length: 65 feet (19.81 m). Beam: 15 feet (4.57 m). Draught: 4 feet (1.22 m).
Propulsion: Gardner 6LXB diesel engine, 127 bhp. Speed: 9 knots, cruising.
Passengers: 100.

KENILWORTH

Kenilworth was built in 1936 at Rowhedge Ironworks, Colchester, as *Hotspur II*, for General Estates, who operated a ferry service between Southampton's Town Quay and Hythe, on the other side of Southampton Water. Originally, she could carry 300 passengers. In 1979, she was sold to Clyde Marine Motoring Ltd and moved to Scotland to operate a ferry service between Gourock and Kilcreggan and Helensburgh. Renamed *Kenilworth*, she operated for twenty-eight years and remained largely unaltered. In April 2007, she was replaced on that ferry service by a newer vessel, and started a new service from Greenock and Helensburgh to Blairmore and Lochgoil. In 2009, she was sold and moved to Inverness, reportedly for further service.

Gross tonnage: 44. Length: 60 feet (18.3 m).
Propulsion: twin Kelvin R6 diesel engines.
Passengers: 127.

Kenilworth as a Clyde ferry. (National Historic Ships)

NORTHERN BELLE

Northern Belle was built as the steam ferry *Armadillo* by Rogers Boatyard, of Cremyll, Cornwall, for the Earl of Mount Edgecumbe's estate, which had, since 1885, operated the ferry service between Cremyll Quay and Admiral's Hard, Plymouth. After the death of the 5th Earl in 1944, the descent ceased and ownership of the vessel passed to the Millbrook Steamboat & Trading Co. In 1946-47, a rebuild by Mashford, Cremyll, (the yard previously owned by Rogers) involved the replacement of the steam engine by a diesel, and the vessel was renamed *Northern Belle*. In 1980, Dart Pleasure Craft took over Millbrook Steamboat & Trading Co. In 1985, the vessel was sold to Tamar Cruising and continued to provide the ferry service until 2009. Then the contract was lost and the future of *Northern Belle* was placed in doubt.

Gross tonnage: 25. Length: 66 feet. (20.1 m).
Propulsion: diesel engine.
Passengers: 157.

Northern Belle in service as a Cremyll ferry. (National Historic Ships)

YARMOUTH BELLE

This interesting vessel was built as a passenger steamer in 1892 by Thomas Bradley, Southtown, Great Yarmouth, in 1892, on his own account, but was subsequently sold to the Great Yarmouth & Gorleston Steamboat Co. *Yarmouth Belle* was mainly used on the Yarmouth to Norwich service on the River Yare, but occasionally ran to St Olaves on the River Waveney and elsewhere on the Broads. In 1946, she was sold to Henry Hastings of Kingston-on-Thames, who in 1947 converted her to diesel using a 1933 engine. In 1955, she passed to Thames Launches and had several other owners before being purchased by her present owners, Turk Launches, in 1988. She was later completely rebuilt and restored at the Turk boatyard in Sunbury-on-Thames: the paddle wheels and funnel are dummies. Her present diesel engine was installed in 1997. She is based at Kingston-on-Thames and is used for cruises and charters including wedding receptions and corporate hospitality. Her plush, Victorian-style lower saloon can accommodate 125, whilst the upper saloon seats thirty-two.

Gross tonnage: 48. Length: 82 feet (25 m). Beam: 19.67 feet (6. m). Draught: 3.3 feet (1.01 m).
Propulsion: six-cylinder Perkins Sabre diesel engine, 130 bhp, single screw.

CHAPTER 4

Steam Tugs

CANNING

A good example of a postwar steam tug, *Canning* was built in 1954 by Cochrane & Sons, of Selby, for the Alexandra Towing Co. Ltd. Her oil-burning engine was manufactured by C. D. Holmes & Co. Ltd, Hull. Two sister tugs, *Waterloo* and *Wallesey*, also completed in 1954, were coal-fired: *Canning* was the first oil-burning tug to be built for the company. For the next five years, all of the company's other new tugs were of similar design and appearance to her, before being superseded by motor tugs. Alexandra Towing operated tug fleets at Liverpool, Swansea, Port Talbot and Southampton, and as her name suggests, *Canning* was based at Liverpool – until being transferred to Swansea in 1966. Her main duties at both ports were towing and berthing large ships in the harbours and docks, but barge towage and coastal towage were also undertaken. She became the last steam tug to operate in the Bristol Channel, serving until 1974. In December 1974, she was acquired by Swansea City Council, with the aid of a 50 per cent grant from the Science Museum, for the Swansea Maritime Museum. *Canning* is now part of the National Waterfront Museum (at Swansea), on display but not open to the public.

Gross tonnage: 200. Length: 103.6 feet (31.58 m). Beam: 30 feet (9.14 m).
Draught: 12 feet (3.66 m).
Propulsion: triple-expansion steam engine, oil-fired Scotch boiler, 950 ihp, single screw. Bunkers: 50 tons of heavy oil fuel.
Crew: 7.

CERVIA

There was an urgent need for intermediate-sized tugs during the Second World War and about 144 were built between 1941 and 1946 for the Ministry of War Transport. There were several types, varying in size from 129 to 295 gross tons, and their designs were based on successful pre-war tugs. They were given 'Empire' names, as was the practice for war-built merchant ships in Britain. *Empire Raymond* was launched on 21 January 1946 by Alexander Hall & Co.

Left: Canning seen in 1992 at Swansea Maritime Museum. (Chris Allen)

Below: Cervia in service with International Towing Ltd. (Martin Stevens)

Ltd, Aberdeen (who also built her engines), and completed on 30 April 1946. Her type was based on the design of the *Foremost* of 1928. She was handed over to Townsend Bros Ferries for onward delivery.

In December 1946, *Empire Raymond* was sold to William Watkins Ltd, a London tug company, and renamed *Cervia*. For two years, she was employed on towing duties between ports on both sides of the English Channel before moving to be based at Gravesend. On 1 February 1950, an amalgamation of towing companies put her ownership under Ship Towage (London) Ltd but she retained her Watkins colours. On 26 October 1954, she was assisting with the undocking of the P. & O. liner *Arcadia* stern first, when, to avoid collision with another vessel, *Arcadia* put her engines ahead and pulled the *Cervia* sideways so that the tug capsized and sank, with the loss of her master and four crew. The steam tug *Challenge* (see below) rescued three survivors. *Cervia* was raised two days later and taken to Ramsgate (where Watkins had a repair yard) for a refit. On 27 January 1969, further rationalisation of companies made her part of London Tugs Ltd.

In 1971, she was laid up at Sheerness and was sold in the following year to Michael List Brain, ostensibly for preservation under the aegis of the Medway Maritime Trust. However, after a refit, *Cervia* returned to towing service in 1974, working in the North Sea and elsewhere on coastal towage. A new company, International Towing Ltd, was formed and owned several tugs based at Ramsgate. *Cervia* remained in service with that company until 1983, her final duties being as port tug for the new cross-channel ferry service at Ramsgate, assisting in adverse weather conditions. She was laid up at Ramsgate and, in July 1985, was loaned to Ramsgate Maritime Museum, run by the East Kent Maritime Trust. She was refitted and repainted in the Watkins colours, berthed in Smeaton's historic dry dock, and opened to the public. In the mid-1990s, her engine was restored to full working order. More recently, her condition has deteriorated and the Steam Museum Trust has launched an appeal for her restoration.

Gross tonnage: 233. Length: 105.2 feet (32.1 m). Beam: 27.1 feet (8.3 m). Draught: 11.7 feet (3.57 m).
Propulsion: three-cylinder triple-expansion steam engine, oil-fired, 900 ihp, single screw.
Crew: 8.

CHALLENGE

Challenge is the last surviving example of a large purpose-built Thames ship-handling tug. She was built in 1931 by Alexander Hall & Co. Ltd, of Aberdeen, for the Elliott Steam Tug Co. Ltd (who operated her until 1950). Her engine was also built by Hall, whilst her boiler was by Palmer's Shipbuilding & Iron Co. Ltd, of Hebburn. *Challenge* spent her entire working life based on the Thames, though

Challenge at the Trafalgar 200 International Fleet Review at Spithead in June 2005. Note that she has a 20-mm Oerlikon gun mounted on the flying bridge. (Author)

her duties sometimes took her further afield, to Holland, Belgium, France, Scotland and the South Coast of England. She passed through two further ownerships: Ship Towage (London) Ltd (from 1950 to 1969) and London Tugs (1969-74).

She was one of the Dunkirk Little Ships engaged in the evacuation of Allied troops from France in May and June 1940. On 31 May, she worked at Dunkirk berthing vessels in the harbour during the evacuation and, the following day, towed small craft to Dunkirk to evacuate troops. At one point, she towed a disabled destroyer loaded with troops back to port. She was also involved in duties at Dover around this time, assisting ships which were engaged in the Dunkirk operation. After returning to the Thames, she was fitted with a flying bridge to mount an Oerlikon cannon, and a forebridge for two Lewis guns. Her work in 1941 included towing Maunsell anti-aircraft towers out into the Thames estuary, and in 1944, towing parts of the Mulberry harbours used in the D-Day landings. On 3 July 1944, she was damaged by a V1 flying bomb in the Royal Albert Dock and was repaired at Rotherhithe. After the war, she continued in Thames service and was converted from coal to oil firing at Sheerness in 1964. In about 1971, she was laid up at Gravesend, having been the last steam tug to serve on the Thames.

In 1973, *Challenge* was sold to Taylor Woodrow Ltd for preservation at St Katharine's Yacht Haven, near Tower Bridge, and was berthed there as a static exhibit. By 1993, her condition had deteriorated badly and the Dunkirk Little

Ships Restoration Trust was formed to save her. With support from Sun Tugs and Tilbury Docks, *Challenge* was moved to Tilbury Docks and work started on her restoration. This has been completed and she has been returned to steaming condition: she was present at the Trafalgar 200 Spithead Review in 2005. There are plans to exhibit her as part of a new heritage centre at Southampton, together with *Calshot* and the harbour defence motor launch *Medusa*.

Gross registered tonnage: 238. Length: 110 feet (33.5 m). Beam: 26.25 feet (8 m). Draught: 14 feet (4.3 m).
Propulsion: triple-expansion steam reciprocating engine, 1,150 ihp, single screw. Crew: 9. Bunkers: 110 tons oil fuel.

DANIEL ADAMSON

A fine surviving example of the steam tug/tender, dual-purpose vessels, which combined towing capabilities with passenger accommodation, *Daniel Adamson* is one of only two tug/tenders to survive in the UK (the other being the *Calshot*), and the only one to retain her original steam power. She was built as the *Ralph Brocklebank* in 1903 by the Tranmere Bay Development Co., Birkenhead, (who also built her engines) for the Shropshire Union Canal & Railway Co., to operate a barge-towing service between Ellesmere Port and Liverpool, whilst her passenger facility was used for a scheduled cross-river service. The passenger service continued until 1915, and in 1921, she was sold to the Manchester Ship Canal Co. together with her two sister ships.

Daniel Adamson in 1990 at Liverpool, where she is undergoing restoration. (Chris Allen)

Daniel Adamson in 1981, in service with the Manchester Ship Canal Co., showing the passenger saloon on her promenade deck. (Daniel Adamson Preservation Society)

The new owners made use of her passenger carrying capability by offering cruises from Manchester to Eastham, though her primary duties were as a tug on the Manchester Ship Canal. In 1936, the vessel was renamed *Daniel Adamson* in honour of the Manchester Ship Canal Company's first chairman, following a refit in which her bridge was raised, the promenade deck was extended to the ship's sides, and the passenger accommodation was upgraded in Art Deco style. This enabled her to take on the additional role of the company directors' inspection vessel and hospitality venue. In 1953, her coal-fired boiler was replaced with a new three-furnace Scotch boiler, also coal-fired, a new funnel was fitted, and the wheelhouse was fully enclosed. In 1986, she was laid up and berthed at the Boat Museum, Ellesmere Port. By 2004, *Daniel Adamson* was in poor condition and was rescued for restoration and taken to the Clarence Graving Dock, Liverpool, for a hull survey, sandblasting and painting. She is now berthed in the Sandon Dock, Liverpool, and is being restored by the *Daniel Adamson* Preservation Society. The society plans to return her to active service, carrying up to 100 passengers. Permission has been gained for her to operate from Liverpool Cruise Liner Terminal, and the hope is to complete restoration in 2011 and begin cruises in 2012.

Gross tonnage: 173. Length: 110 feet (33.5 m). Beam: 24.5 feet (7.47 m). Draught: 6 feet (1.83 m).
Propulsion: two two-cylinder compound steam engines, 583 ihp, twin screw.
Crew: 7. Bunkers: 28 tons (21 tons from 1936 onwards).

JOHN H. AMOS

The first steam tugs were paddle tugs, and although screw tugs largely superseded them, the type continued to be built until 1931, when the last, *John H. Amos*, was built for the Tees Conservancy Commissioners by Bow McLachlan & Co. Ltd, Paisley (who also built her engines and boilers). She was named after an octogenarian Secretary to the Commissioners, John Hetherington Amos. Before her completion, the builders went into liquidation and the tug was completed by the liquidators. However, the boilers installed could not supply enough steam and the maximum speed attained was 11 knots instead of the intended 13 knots. She was powered by two compound diagonal engines, one for each paddle wheel – so that each wheel could be operated independently, giving her considerable manoeuvrability. The paddle wheels could also be worked together by means of a clutch.

John H. Amos was completed in February 1931, but the commissioners would not accept her due to the speed problem, and it was a further two years before she was finally accepted. She was given a passenger certificate for 144 passengers to make her more useful, and took the Commissioners and their official guests on excursions. She worked on the Tees, serving the ports of Middlesbrough, Hartlepool and Stockton, and her duties included towing dredgers and taking their associated hopper barges to and from the dumping grounds, and taking fresh water to ships. In January 1967, her ownership passed to the Tees and Hartlepool Port Authority. Her new owners withdrew her from service almost immediately and, in 1968, donated her to the Middlesbrough Museum Service. Some work was done in re-plating part of the hull at Middlesbrough, but she was then laid up at Stockton Quay from December 1971, and only limited maintenance was carried out. A plan to restore her to museum status failed, and in 1976, she was sold to Martin Stevens and Michael List Brain of the Medway Maritime Trust.

John H. Amos in International Towing Ltd (ITL) colours, sheltering on the Humber in March 1976 while en route from the Tees to Chatham. (Martin Stevens)

The steam tug *Cervia* towed the *John H. Amos* to Chatham in March 1976: both vessels were by then painted in the livery of International Towing Ltd and *John H. Amos* was renamed *Hero*. The paddle tug (which subsequently reverted to her original name) successively occupied several different berths at Chatham, ending up on a disused slipway, where she sat on a lump of concrete and her hull was flooded. For many years, her condition deteriorated. In 2008, she was lifted onto a pontoon for inspection and restoration, subject to the successful application for grants from the Heritage Lottery Fund.

Gross tonnage: 202. Length: 110 feet (33.5 m). Beam: 43 feet (13.1 m) over paddle wheels. Draught: 11.5 feet (3.5 m).
Propulsion: two diagonal compound steam engines, 500 ihp. Speed: 11 knots. Crew: 6.

KERNE

Originally to have been named *Viking*, this steam tug was purchased by the Admiralty in March 1913, which was also the month of her completion, from her builders, Montrose Shipbuilding Co. Ltd, Montrose. Her steam engine was built by W. V. V. Lidgerwood, of Coatbridge. Renamed *Terrier* by the Admiralty, she was allocated to Chatham Dockyard as a basin tug, as was her sister ship *Tyke*. She was re-boilered in 1935 with a boiler built in Chatham dockyard and continued to work there until 1948.

She was sold on 15 March 1948 to J. P. Knight Ltd, London, and renamed *Kerne*, for duties on the Thames and Medway (kerne is Gaelic for 'foot soldier'). She still had a folding funnel and open navigating platform. However, she was sold on 13 September of the following year to the Straits Steamship Co. Ltd, Liverpool. The tug was modified in 1949 with a non-folding funnel of increased height, an enclosed wheelhouse, a new mast, washports cut in the after bulwarks, and a small whaleback compartment on the deck to house the WC.

Kerne towed barges on the River Mersey, the Manchester Ship Canal and River Weaver systems for the next twenty-two years and, from April 1965, was under the ownership of the Liverpool Lighterage Company Ltd. In April 1971, she was laid up for disposal and sold to the North Western Steam Ship Co. Ltd, a non-profit-making organisation, for preservation in steaming condition – retaining the name *Kerne*. She is usually based at the Merseyside Maritime Museum at Liverpool or at the Boat Museum at Ellesmere Port. She has made voyages to the Isle of Man, North Wales ports, Porthmadog and cruises on the Weaver and Ship Canal Systems.

Gross Registered Tonnage: 62.7. Length: 77 feet (23.5 m). Beam: 18.25 feet (5.6 m). Draught: 9.5 feet (2.9 m).
Propulsion: steam triple-expansion reciprocating engine, 300 ihp, single Scotch boiler, single screw. Speed: 10 knots.

Kerne in service on the Mersey, some time before 1965. (World Ship Society)

The preserved *Kerne*, seen at Acton Bridge. (Chris Allen)

MAYFLOWER

The oldest surviving British tug (and probably the oldest in the world) is the *Mayflower*, which was built of iron in 1861 by Stothert & Marten, of Hotwells, Bristol, for Timothy Hadley, a towage contractor to the Gloucester & Berkeley Canal Co. She had a single-cylinder vertical steam engine, and began work towing small sailing vessels, timber rafts and canal and river boats on the canal, working between Gloucester and the old entrance to the canal north of Sharpness, replacing horses in this task. In 1874, with the building of the Sharpness Docks, the canal company was renamed the Sharpness New Docks & Gloucester & Birmingham Navigation Co., and purchased the *Mayflower* and other tugs from Hadley. She continued to work on the canal, now working with larger steam ships that could navigate to Gloucester, or with lighters filled by the larger traffic into Sharpness.

In 1899, a new vertical compound engine, boiler, funnel and propeller were installed (all of which except the boiler remain in her), making *Mayflower* powerful enough to work in the Severn Estuary. The boiler was replaced in 1909. In 1906, she was modified with a hinged funnel, to allow her to work more easily up stream on the River Severn as far as Worcester and Stourport. Originally, she had a steering position astern of the engine-room skylight, so that the skipper could operate the engine via long levers as well as steer: this had been replaced

The restored *Mayflower* in steam in the Floating Harbour at Bristol, with passengers on board, in 2006. (Chris Allen)

by a waist-height steering shelter forward of the funnel. In 1921, a higher deck and cut-away bulwarks changed her appearance again, and in the late 1930s, a wooden wheelhouse replaced the steering shelter; some time after this the bulwarks were replaced.

By the end of the Second World War, *Mayflower* had been relegated to light duties, and spent most of the war period as a tender to the canal dredger, towing the mud hopper barges filled by the dredger to the discharge point. In 1948, she was passed to the British Waterways Board and retained as a reserve vessel for busy periods. In the winter of 1962/63, the canal froze and *Mayflower* was once again used for ship towage on the canal. This was her swansong, for in 1964, she was laid up and was sold two years later. She lay neglected and, in 1977, sank in Gloucester Docks. She was refloated and was sold in 1981 to Bristol Industrial Museum for restoration to steaming condition, which was completed by 1987. Since then, *Mayflower* has been exhibited outside the museum and has also offered trips under steam in Bristol Harbour, carrying up to twelve passengers. In 2006, the Industrial Museum closed but, after a transformation, is to reopen as the Museum of Bristol. At the time of writing, *Mayflower* is undergoing a major refit and should be steaming again when the new museum opens in 2011.

Gross registered tonnage: 32. Length: 65 feet (19.8 m). Beam: 12 feet (3.66 m). Draught: 7 feet (2.13 m).
Propulsion: vertical compound steam engine, single screw.
Crew: 3.

PORTWEY

A fine example of a small steam coastal and river tug, the twin screw, coal-fired *Portwey* is maintained in steaming condition and is normally to be found berthed in the West India Docks, London. She was ordered from Harland & Wolff, Govan, in October 1926 for barge and collier towing duties with the Portland & Weymouth Coaling Co. at Weymouth – her name being derived from the company name. Her engines were built by W. & D. Henderson, Glasgow, and she was launched on 10 August 1927 and completed on 28 April 1928. In addition to being equipped for towing, *Portwey* was fitted with water tanks, of 33 tons capacity, to take fresh water (as well as other supplies) to ships.

In 1938, she was sold to G. H. Collins & Co. Ltd of Dartmouth, still under the ownership of the previous holding company, Evans & Reid. In 1942, she came under the control of the US Army at Dartmouth: her duties included towing damaged vessels back to port. After the war, *Portwey* returned to Weymouth (with the Channel Coaling Co., another Evans & Reid subsidiary) until August 1951, when she sold to the Falmouth Dock & Engineering Co. Ltd at Falmouth and was used on towage duties in Falmouth harbour for fourteen years. In 1965, she was used on a contract at Holyhead and then withdrawn from service.

Portwey underway at sea. (World Ship Society)

Portwey on display at West India Quay in 2008. (Author)

In 1967, she was bought for preservation by Richard Dobson of Stoke Gabriel, on the River Dart, and steamed there from Holyhead. She took up moorings on the Dart, and for fifteen years, a dedicated group maintained and restored her, and she was regularly steamed in the summer months. In 1982, she was sold to the Maritime Trust (who had previously assisted with her restoration) and steamed to London in June of that year to join the historic ship collection in St Katharine Docks. In June 2000, she was chartered to the Steam Tug *Portwey* Trust, which was formed to continue the programme of renovation and operation of the vessel. She is still occasionally steamed.

Gross registered tonnage: 94. Length: 80.5 feet (24.5 m). Beam: 18 feet (5.5 m). Draught: 9 feet (2.74 m).
Propulsion: two-cylinder compound steam reciprocating engine, 330 ihp, twin screw. One Scotch boiler with twin furnaces (coal-fired). Speed: 9.75 knots. Crew: 8.

TID CLASS

The TID-class tug was a standard wartime type built in large numbers. The first were ordered in 1942 to replace war losses and, in all, 182 had been built by 1946. They were ordered by the Ministry of War Transport for both government service and charter to commercial operators. One of their roles was to assist with the Normandy invasion preparations along the French and Belgian coasts, towing barges and working with elements of the Mulberry harbours. To minimise the demands on shipyard capacity, the design was simplified to allow the construction of prefabricated sections by inland steel fabricators, and utilised a hard chine hull to help in this regard. The eight sections (each of up to 6 tons) for each tug were then transported by road and assembled and welded together at a shipyard – mostly by Richard Dunston Ltd, at Thorne and Hessle, or – in the case of twenty-three tugs – by William Pickersgill & Co., Sunderland. The boiler, engine and superstructure were added after the launching. All TIDs were built with an open navigating platform, though later, many had enclosed wheelhouses fitted.

During peak production, one tug was being turned out every four and a half days. Like the VIC-class coastal lighters (q.v.), they were steam-powered: the first ninety units were coal-fired, whilst the later craft were oil-fired. The origin of the TID acronym is obscure, and explanations have included Tug Invasion Duty, Tug Inshore Duties, Tug Intermediate Design, or more simply, Tiddler. Many were assigned to naval dockyards and continued in postwar naval service, some until the mid-seventies. In 1963, for example, sixteen were still in the Admiralty's Port Auxiliary Service at six different dockyards. Two of these – *TID 164* and *TID 172* have survived to the present day in the hands of preservation enthusiasts, and are based at Chatham Historic Dockyard and Mistley, Essex, respectively.

TID 164 at Chatham Historic Dockyard's Anchor Wharf in 2006. (Author)

TID 172 at Stellendam, Holland, in 2004. (Max Brown)

TID 164 was completed on 28 November 1945 by Pickersgill and was in naval service at Port Edgar, on the Forth estuary, attached to HMS *Lochinvar*, the minesweeper base. In 1947, she was chartered by the Port of London Authority to work in the London Docks, returning in the next year to the Firth of Forth to work at Rosyth Dockyard. In December 1962, *TID 164* was placed in reserve at Rosyth and, five years later, re-entered service there. In June 1974, she was sold to the Medway Maritime Museum for preservation and steamed to the Medway. In 1975, she was renamed *Hercules* to operate on towage for International Towing Ltd, a commercial venture of the Medway Maritime Trust. This work took her to London, Rye, the Clyde and the Caledonian Canal and ended in 1978. She reverted to her original name and, whilst berthed at Chatham, sank at her moorings when a drain plug in the bottom of her hull broke. In 2009, she again sank at her berth and was raised, but a requirement was made that she be removed from Chatham Historic Dockyard.

TID 172 was built by Henry Scarr Ltd, Hessle, (which had been taken over by Dunston) and completed in 1946. Her oil-fired engine was by J. Dickinson & Sons Ltd, Sunderland. She was allocated to the Nore Command under the Naval Officer in Charge at Lowestoft, and was given the name *Martello*. On 11 July 1946, she reverted to the name *TID 172* with a civilian crew. On 20 October 1946, she was transferred to the Civil Engineer-in-Chief, Chatham, becoming *W92* (which indicates that she was operated by the Ministry of Works). On 1 October 1959, she was allocated to the Port Auxiliary Service at Chatham and was once again renamed *TID 172*. She was sold to T. W. Ward Ltd, Grays, on 9 July 1973 for demolition, but was reprieved through her onward sale to Mr B. Pearce of Maldon for preservation. She is now owned by Max Brown at Mistley in Essex and is steamed at least once each season.

Brent, ex-*TID 159*, now based at Maldon, was built by Pickersgill in 1945, and did not see naval service. In 1946, she was sold to the Port of London Authority, who renamed her *Brent*, and served in the Dredging Department and dock system until she was laid up in 1969. She was the last steam tug to be employed in London's enclosed dock system. In 1970, she was sold to a ship-breaker but was saved by a private buyer, Ron Hall, in 1971.

Another TID still in steam is *Tommi*, ex-*TID 35*, which was built in 1943. She has been in Finland since 1946 and now burns wood.

Gross registered tonnage: 54. Length: 65 feet (19.8 m). Beam: 17 feet (5.18 m). Draught: 6 feet (1.8 m).
Propulsion: two-cylinder compound steam reciprocating engine, 220 ihp, single boiler, single screw.
Speed: 8.5 knots. Bunkers: 8 tons coal or 8.6 tons oil.
Crew: 6.

CHAPTER 5

Motor Tugs

BROCKLEBANK

One of five motor tugs built by W. J. Yarwood & Sons Ltd, Northwich, between 1962 and 1965 for Alexandra Towing Co. Ltd, Liverpool, *Brocklebank* was launched in 1964 and completed in February 1965. She was mainly used for ship handling at Liverpool, but had occasional duties at Heysham, Larne and Barrow. In 1989, she was purchased by Merseyside Maritime Museum and manned by experienced mariners on behalf of the Friends of the National Museums Liverpool. Normally berthed in the Albert Dock next to the maritime museum, she also attends maritime festivals around the coast of the United Kingdom.

Gross tonnage: 172. Length: 103 feet (31.4 m). Beam: 27.1 feet (8.26 m). Draught: 12.5 feet (3.81 m).
Propulsion: two eight-cylinder Crossley diesel engines, 1,200 bhp, single screw. Speed: 12 knots.

CALSHOT

The port of Southampton had a requirement for tug/tenders to attend to liners anchored in Cowes Roads, and *Calshot* was completed in 1930 to fulfil this role in the fleet of the Southampton, Isle of Wight & South of England Royal Mail Steam Packet Company (or Red Funnel as it became known). She was built by John I. Thornycroft & Co. Ltd, of Woolston, Southampton, launched on 4 November 1929, and fitted with triple-expansion steam engines, which were also built by Thornycroft. Principally used for local towing and tender duties, *Calshot* also served as a relief vessel on the Southampton to Ryde excursion service, and, on occasions, for salvage work in the Channel. On 16 December 1940, she was requisitioned by the Admiralty and sent to Scapa Flow to tender the Home Fleet at its anchorage. She reverted to the Red Ensign in 1942 (though some records say she remained under Admiralty control until 1 September 1945) and went to the Clyde to tender the 'Queens' and other liners (which were on trooping duties) at the Tail o' the Bank. In May 1944, she returned to Southampton for D-Day duties.

Brocklebank on display at the Albert Dock, Liverpool, in 2009. (Author)

Calshot in steam off Hythe, on Southampton Water, in the early sixties. (Michael Lennon)

Galway Bay on her return to Southampton on 8 June 1988. (Michael Lennon)

Calshot photographed from the *QE2* in Berth 39 at Southampton Docks on 11 November 2008, showing her funnel extended again. (Janette McCutcheon)

After an extensive refit, *Calshot* rejoined the Red Funnel fleet in June 1946 and continued in service until 1964, when replaced by a new motor tug/tender of the same name. She was sold to Port & Liner Services (Ireland) Ltd, a subsidiary of the Holland America Line, and renamed *Galway Bay*. Converted to diesel propulsion, with a shorter funnel, she was based at Galway for tender work to the liners *Maasdam* and *Ryndam*, and local excursion services. By 1971, she was owned by Galway Ferries Ltd and used as a ferry between Galway and the Aran Islands, as well as excursions, until the end of the 1985 season.

In 1986, she was bought by Southampton City Council to be the centrepiece of a proposed maritime museum. This scheme did not proceed, and she remained in Southampton Docks. In 1997, the Tug Tender *Calshot* Trust was set up with the aim of restoring *Calshot* to her 1930s profile, including heightening her funnel. Limited work has been undertaken, but further progress is contingent on successful application for grants. It is planned that she will become an exhibit at a new heritage centre in Southampton, together with *Challenge* and the harbour defence motor launch *Medusa*.

Gross tonnage: 684. Length: 147 feet (44.8 m). Beam: 33 feet (10.06 m). Draught: 12 feet (3.66 m).
Propulsion (as built): triple-expansion steam reciprocating engines, 1,500 ihp, twin screws. (Since converted to Bolnes diesel propulsion.)
Passengers (as built): 566.

GARNOCK

The motor tug *Garnock* was built in 1956 by George Brown & Co. Ltd, of Greenock, for the Irvine Harbour Company, a subsidiary of ICI. Launched on 4 October 1956, her hull was partially riveted and partly welded. Her engines were manufactured by Lister Blackstone Marine Ltd, Bursley. She was registered at Irvine for operation in the Clyde estuary, towing ships which loaded and unloaded explosives at the nearby ICI (Nobel Explosives) works. Latterly, she was also used to dump explosives in the estuary.

In February 1984, she was severely damaged by an explosion while dumping explosives west of Ardrossan. The Troon lifeboat was called to the scene and towed the tug to Troon. Repairing the damage to her aft end and propeller was not an economic proposition, and after essential work, she was donated to the Scottish Maritime Museum and is now on static display at Irvine.

Gross tonnage: 78. Length: 78 feet 5 inches (23.9 m). Beam: 21 feet 11 inches (6.68 m). Draught: 8 feet 2 inches (2.49 m).
Propulsion: Lister Blackstone diesel, 324 bhp. Single screw. Speed: 9.25 knots.

Garnock on display at the Scottish Maritime Museum, Irvine. (National Historic Ships)

John King underway in the Floating Harbour at Bristol, with passengers on board, in 2007.
(Chris Jones)

JOHN KING

Built in 1935 for C. J. King & Sons, Bristol tug operators since 1859, by Charles Hill & Sons Ltd, at Bristol, *John King* was a motor tug used for ship towage on the River Avon and in Bristol Docks until 1970. During the Blitz of 1940, she was employed for seventeen days fighting fires at the Pembroke Dock oil installations and, on her way back to Bristol, was attacked by a German aircraft. Her last job, on 6 July 1970, was to manoeuvre the SS *Great Britain* into the Great Western Dock. She was then sold to F. A. Ashmead & Son for further service on the Severn and renamed *Peter Leigh*. Her work involved towing African hardwood logs in barges from Avonmouth across the River Severn to Lydney. In 1978, she was sold to Bristol Commercial Ships and renamed *Pride*, and towed as far as Southampton and Milford haven. In 1986, she was renamed *Durdham*. In 1995, she was purchased by the Bristol Industrial Museum and reverted to her original name. She has been kept in working condition and has operated passenger trips at Bristol, and will continue to be located there as part of the new Museum of Bristol.

Gross tonnage: 49. Length: 68.5 feet (20.9 m). Beam: 17 feet (5.18 m). Draught: 8.5 feet (2.59 m).
Propulsion: Lister Blackstone diesel engine, 300 bhp, single screw.

KENT

This motor tug was built by Richards' Ironworks Co. Ltd, Lowestoft, in 1948 for J. P. Knight Ltd, London. At first, she worked on ship handling at the Medway ports of Rochester, Chatham and Sheerness, but later worked elsewhere in the UK, on coastal towage and other duties, with spells in Scotland and Ireland under contract to various civil engineering companies. When J. P. Knight opened their Caledonian branch at Invergordon, *Kent* was there to pioneer a new coastal towage service. In 1952, when the BP refinery at the Isle of Grain was opened, *Kent* had the bow line on *British Skill*, the first tanker to unload there, as she approached the jetty and berthed. *Kent* was taken out of service in 1987 and lay on the Medway in semi-preserved condition. In 1995, she was acquired by the South Eastern Tug Society for restoration and preservation. In January 1999, she moved under her own power for the first time since 1987. *Kent* is maintained in working condition, based at No. 1 Basin, Chatham, and often attends maritime heritage events – including visits to St Malo, Ostend, Dover, Yarmouth, Harwich, and the Thames and Medway ports. She is a good example of an early postwar motor tug and is of riveted construction.

Gross tonnage: 121. Length: 81.3 feet (24.8 m). Beam: 22 feet (6.7 m). Draught: 9.5 feet (2.9 m).
Propulsion: five-cylinder British Polar diesel engine, 880 bhp, single screw.

Kent seen in service in about 1965. (Author's collection)

KNOCKER WHITE

This tug was built in 1924 by T. van Duivendijk, Lekkerkerk, Netherlands, as *Cairnrock*, for Harrisons Lighterage Company, London, and was originally steam-powered. She later passed into the ownership of W. E. White & Sons, Rotherhithe, and in 1960 was renamed with the nickname of one of the White family. She was converted to diesel power with the installation of Petters engines, and alterations were made to both the funnel and wheelhouse. In November 1982, she was sold for scrap, and parts of her engines were removed. In 1984, she was reprieved and became part of the collection of the Museum of London Docklands. She is berthed at West India Quay, close to the museum, together with the 'tosher' (small Thames lighterage tug) *Varlet*. (*Varlet* was built in 1937 by James Pollock & Sons, Faversham, for Vokins & Co. Ltd, and worked extensively in the West India and Royal Docks until the early 1980s.) Restoration work on both vessels has been supported by the Heritage Lottery Fund.

Gross tonnage: 90. Length: 77.2 feet (23.5 m). Beam: 20 feet (6.1 m).
Propulsion: Petters diesel, single screw.

SEVERN PROGRESS

Built in 1931 by Charles Hill & Sons Ltd, Bristol, for the Severn Canal Carrying Co., based at Gloucester, and originally named *Progress*, this tug was renamed *Severn Progress* in 1933. She was completed with a 100-bhp Kromhout semi-diesel engine, which was later replaced by a Lister diesel. Steering was from

Knocker White on display at West India Quay, London, in 2008. (Author)

Severn Progress at Gloucester in 2009. (Author)

an open well, and later a wheelhouse was added. *Severn Progress* was mainly used for towing barges and narrow boats between Gloucester and Worcester, sometimes extending to Stourport. These barges and canal boats carried cargoes that had been brought on ships to Bristol and Avonmouth. The tug was based at the Ship Inn and tows were normally picked up after they had passed through the Gloucester lock. Narrow boats bound for the Midlands would be left at Worcester to pass into the canal. After nationalisation of the canals in 1948, the tug became part of the British Waterways fleet and continued towing on the Severn until commercial traffic died out in the late 1960s. She moved to the Kennet & Avon Canal to assist with maintenance work between Hanham Lock and Bath. In 1991, she was acquired by the British Waterways Museum and is normally berthed in the Gloucester Docks.

Gross tonnage: not known. Length: 41.5 feet (12.65 m). Beam: 11 feet (3.35 m). Draught: 6 feet (1.83 m).
Propulsion: Lister diesel engine.
Crew: 2.

THOMAS

Thomas was built as *Oner II* by Cochrane & Sons Ltd, Selby, in 1937 and was purchased in 1938 by the Admiralty (and renamed *C10*) as their first motor tug, for use on fleet fuelling duties at Portsmouth. During the Second World War, she assisted with the laying of the Pluto oil pipeline to France, and with the movement of Mulberry harbour sections. In 1958, she was renamed *Destiny* and was part of the Port Auxiliary Service from 1959, remaining on her previous duties at the Forton Oil Depot, Gosport until 1961 when was replaced by the new motor tug *Alice*. On 13 November 1963, *Destiny* was sold to H. G. Pounds, Portsmouth, who later resold her to Husbands Shipyard Ltd, Marchwood, for commercial service under the name *Affluence*. By 1988, she was owned by Star Tug & Marine Co. Ltd and used for film work. In 1991, she was sold to a Swansea businessman, Ken Thomas, who refitted her and renamed her *Thomas*, and is now preserved at Port Talbot.

Gross registered tonnage: 89. Length: 80 feet (24.38 m). Beam: 21 feet (6.4 m). Propulsion: diesel engine, 450 bhp, single screw. Speed: 10 knots.

WENDY ANN

In 1934, Alexander Hall & Co. Ltd, Aberdeen, built the motor tug *Brodstone* for Frederick Leyland Ltd of Liverpool, although the vessel was employed in London. In 1935, she was renamed *Evelene Brodstone* upon transfer to a subsidiary

Thomas seen here when named *Destiny*, as a Port Auxiliary Service tug, in 1960. (World Ship Society)

A recent photo of *Thomas*. (National Historic Ships)

Wendy Ann taking a tow into Ramsey, in August 2009. (John Williamson)

company, Blackfriars Lighterage. Her service on the Thames continued in 1946 when she was sold to Gaselee & Son Ltd and renamed *Vespa*. In 1953, she was run down and sunk in Gallions Reach by the Swedish freighter *Malmo*. After salvage, her original Mirrlees, Bickerton & Day diesel was replaced by 525-bhp British Polar diesel. In 1965, Gaselee sold their four largest tugs, including *Vespa*, to Ship Towage (London) Ltd, which became London Tugs Ltd in 1969. Harry Rose, a Poole tug operator, purchased the tug in 1970 but did not rename her until four years later, when she became *Wendy Ann*. Her engine was replaced in 1972 with a Blackstone diesel. The tug's duties at Poole included assisting colliers, and later coastal tankers, at the town's power station, assisting coasters and ferries, maintaining the sewerage outfall buoys, and towing hopper barges for the Poole Harbour Commissioners' dredger when their tug was not available. In 1981, *Wendy Ann* was sold to the harbour commissioners and continued in their service until 1996 when she was sold to the Laxey Towing Co. in the Isle of Man, which still operates her. She is employed berthing ships in Douglas harbour and towing the harbour's hopper barge, and at Ramsey Harbour.

Gross tonnage: 72. Length: 75.5 feet (23 m). Beam: 18.7 feet (5.7 m). Draught: 9.84 feet (3 m).
Propulsion: Blackstone diesel, 600 bhp.

CHAPTER 6
Cargo Vessels and Tankers

BASUTO

Basuto is a rare surviving 'true' Clyde puffer and can be seen at the British Waterways' Boat Museum at Ellesmere Port. Clyde puffers evolved as small steamships that could fit in the Forth & Clyde Canal locks, and for this, they had to be no longer than 66 feet (20 m). The term puffer derived from the fact that steam was exhausted directly from the second cylinder of the compound steam engine, rather than being directed into a condenser. The steam did not need to be condensed and reused because fresh water could be drawn from the canal. The engine produced a characteristic puff of steam from the funnel on each piston stroke, and also itself emitted a puffing noise. Puffers were also used on inshore services around the Firth of Clyde, Loch Fyne, and the Western Isles, and usually had a flat bottom so that they could be beached to unload at low tide at remote locations that lacked a pier. They typically had bluff bows, a single mast with derrick forward of the hold, and an open navigating platform (later enclosed in a wheelhouse) abaft the funnel. Two of the crew of three were accommodated in a cabin in the fo'c'sle, whilst the captain had a small cabin aft.

Basuto was built in 1902 of steel by William Jacks & Co., Port Dundas, Scotland, for that company's own use on the Firth & Clyde Canal. In 1919, she was sold to J. Kelly & Co., Belfast, a coal-merchant. In the 1920s, she was acquired by Cooper & Sons, of Widnes, and was converted into a dumb barge to carry sand and gravel. Later, she was purchased by the Manchester Dry Docks Ltd and was returned to steam with a new engine. Her boiler dates from 1961 and was manufactured by the Cradley Boiler Company. In 1981, she was acquired by the Boat Museum at Ellesmere Port and placed on display there.

Gross tonnage: 64. Length: 66 feet (20.1 m). Beam: 15.74 feet (4.8 m). Draught: 9 feet (2.74 m).
Propulsion: two-cylinder compound steam engine, single screw.
Crew: 3.

Basuto at the Boat Museum, Ellesmere Port, in 2009. (Author)

Cuddington at the Boat Museum, Ellesmere Port, in 2009. (Author)

CUDDINGTON

Of a type generically known as a Weaver packet, *Cuddington* was built of steel in 1948 by W. J. Yarwood & Sons, Northwich, Cheshire, for Imperial Chemical Industries (ICI). She was named after a village near Northwich and carried chemicals, such as soda ash, from the ICI works at Winnington, near Northwich, down the rivers Weaver and Mersey to Liverpool. She carried on working until the 1970s and, in 1979, went to the Boat Museum, Ellesmere Port, where she is still on display in the lower basin close to *Basuto*.

Gross tonnage: 201. Length: 100 feet (30.5 m). Beam: 22 feet (6.7 m). Draught: 11.25 feet (3.4 m).
Propulsion: Crossley diesel engine, 265 bhp, single screw.

JAMES JACKSON GRUNDY

Another Weaver packet, also built by W. J. Yarwood & Sons Ltd, Northwich, in 1948, *James Jackson Grundy* was the first of five motor vessels built for ICI and was named after the distribution manager of the Alkali Division. She was an adaptation from the last three steam lighters that ICI had commissioned between 1944 and 1946.

A recent view of *James Jackson Grundy*. (National Historic Ships)

From 1948 to 1980, she carried soda between the Winnington and Wallercote works on the River Weaver at Northwich and the Liverpool and Birkenhead docks. In 1980, she became a training ship for the TS *Witch* sea cadets at Northwich and continued as such until 2001. She was then sold and is at Liverpool. In 2007, an appeal fund was set up to bring the vessel back to Northwich as a floating museum and heritage centre, celebrating Yarwood's, ICI and the Weaver Navigation. She had just been docked and surveyed and was said to be in good working order. All her upperworks had been repaired and her main and auxiliary machinery had been thoroughly overhauled.

A sister ship, *Wincham*, was sold in 1983 to the *Wincham* Preservation Trust (affiliated to the Friends of National Museums Liverpool) and preserved for display at a berth in the Albert Dock, next to the Mersey Maritime Museum, Liverpool. She was unceremoniously scrapped in 2009 (after the Friends group was disbanded and she lost her main source of income), causing an outcry that a historic ship had been lost without all avenues being explored to save her.

Gross tonnage: 210. Length: 98 feet (29.8 m). Beam: 22.1 feet (6.74 m). Draught: 10 feet (3.05 m).
Propulsion: Crossley diesel engine, 268 bhp. Speed: 8 knots.

SAFE HAND

Safe Hand was the last steam barge built for service on the Mersey and became the last steam vessel in service with the Lever Brothers fleet. She was built in 1950 by W. J. Yarwood & Sons Ltd, Northwich, as the steam tank barge *Lux* for Lever

Safe Hand, still in commercial service. (National Historic Ships)

Brothers, to carry crude vegetable oils from the Mersey ports to Lever's facility at Port Sunlight. In February 1965, she was converted to diesel at Birkenhead and continued to work for Lever Bros until December 1984, being renamed *Safe Hand* in 1975. Her cargo-carrying facilities are two tanks, capable of storing 232 cubic metres of oil, with heating coils. From 1985 onwards, she worked for Mersey Tanker Lighterage (Logantor Ltd) carrying vegetable oils in Liverpool and Birkenhead docks, and is still in service.

Gross tonnage: 112. Length: 100 feet (30.5 m). Beam: 23 feet (7 m). Draught: 8 feet (2.4 m).
Propulsion: eight-cylinder Bergius Kelvin diesel engine. Speed: 8.5 knots.

VIC CLASS

In August 1939, two Clyde puffers, *Anzac* and *Lascar*, were launched for J. Hay & Sons by Messrs Scotts of Bowling. They were small cargo ships of a type used in the Western Isles of Scotland since late in the nineteenth century (see also *Basuto*). After the outbreak of war, their design was adopted by the Ministry of War Transport for a class of steam coastal lighters which would service ships at naval bases both at home and abroad, carrying a diversity of cargoes including dry stores, water, aviation spirit, ammunition and coal. Sixty-three of this 66-foot type were built and given VIC names and numbers, this acronym meaning victualling inshore craft. They had the traditional puffer appearance with the navigating platform (later often enclosed as a wheelhouse) abaft the funnel, a marked sheer to the deck line, a straight stem, countered stern, and a well-cambered hull profile. Most were steam-powered with coal-firing, so that valuable oil supplies were not needed: however, nine had diesel engines and were used overseas as petrol carriers.

Thirty-five of a larger, 80-foot class were also built, two of which were diesel-powered, whilst the others were coal- or oil-fired steamers. This type had a utilitarian, slab-sided, hard chine hull shape with little sheer, to simplify the plate work, and the funnel was placed abaft the navigating platform (or, later, the wheelhouse).

Surprisingly, both types were largely built in English shipyards, and only one is definitely known to have been built in a Scottish yard. Forty were built by R. Dunston Ltd, Thorne, twenty-five by I. Pimblott & Sons Ltd, Northwich, and the remainder by nine other yards, between 1941 and 1946. Many continued in government service well into the postwar period: in 1963, for example, the Admiralty's Port Auxiliary Service still operated twenty-one of the small type and twenty-two of the larger craft. By 1978, only *VIC 56* and *VIC 65* remained in naval service, and the last of these, *VIC 65*, was sold in 1980 and scrapped. Others carried on even longer in commercial ownership. Five of the 66-foot type and two of the 80-foot type have survived in UK waters.

Advance (formerly *VIC 24*) seen in 2004. (National Historic Ships)

VIC 32 on the Caledonian Canal, near Fort Augustus, in 2000. (Chris Tomlinson)

Above: Spartan in service. (World Ship Society)

Right: Vital Spark, which was built as *VIC 72*, at Bowling Harbour, West Dumbartonshire, in December 2007. Her visit marked the anniversary of the launching of the first Clyde puffer, named *Glasgow*, 150 years earlier. (Lairich Rig)

Bearing the name *Vital Spark*, this puffer is actually the former *VIC 27*, later *Auld Reekie* and more recently renamed *Maggie*, which name is on a board hanging from her side. She is photographed at Ardrishaig in 2008. (Alasdair McNeill)

Of the smaller craft, *Advance* (ex-*VIC 24*) is undergoing restoration at Plymouth. She was built in 1942 by Dunston, and was allocated by the Ministry of War Transport to the Ministry of Supply from 2 December 1942 until 10 May 1943. She was then used by the Admiralty until 31 July 1945, and was then sold out of naval service to Ross Marshall Ltd, Greenock. In April 1949, she was sold and moved to Harwich. In 1956, she was sold to W. C. Allan & Sons, Gillingham, and renamed *Advance*. She was later sold to H. G. Pounds, Portsmouth, who sold her on and she spent many years in Holland. She was bought by the current owner from Husbands Shipyard, Southampton, after extensive restoration.

VIC 32, also built by Dunston, was completed in 1943; her engine was by Crabtree of Great Yarmouth and is still coal-fired. During the war, she is believed to have carried cement, ammunition and aviation fuel, delivering supplies to the fleet in Loch Eil and Scapa Flow. She was renamed *C702* and worked at Rosyth Dockyard after the war. She was sold in December 1963 to Whites, Inverkeithing, to be scrapped, but was sold on to Keith Schellenburg and moved to Whitby for restoration, reverting to her original name. In October 1975, she was purchased by Nick Walker and, in May 1976, steamed to London, where she was restored at St Katharine's Yacht Haven. The hold was converted into accommodation at two levels – the lower one sleeps twelve passengers in six twin or double cabins, and the upper one is a saloon. The hatch boards were raised by 23 inches and windows were fitted in the sides to give a clerestory roof. She was then used by her owner for trips on the Thames and for a cruise to the French Channel coast. In 1978, *VIC 32* sailed via Inverness and the Caledonian Canal to Crinan, on the Sound of Jura, in Argyll and Bute. She offered seven-day cruises from Tarbert to Loch Fyne and the Firth of Clyde, and on the Caledonian Canal, and was operated by Highland Steamboat Holidays Ltd, owned by Nick and Rachel Walker. In 1994, her base moved to Crinan Ferry. In 2004, her boiler failed its annual survey and she ceased operations. The Puffer Preservation Trust was formed to raise funds for a new boiler, and with the help of National Heritage Lottery funding, she was re-boiled in 2006 and returned to service, offering week-long cruises with the renamed Puffer Steamboat Holidays Ltd, still operated by the Walkers.

Spartan (ex-*VIC 18*) was built by J. Hay & Sons, Kirkintilloch, in 1940. *VIC 18* was the only VIC known to have been built in a Scottish yard. After the war, she was sold to her builders, who also operated a puffer fleet, on 24 September 1946, and renamed *Spartan*. She was employed in carrying coal and general cargoes around the Firth of Clyde and as far as Mull, Iona and Islay. She was motorised with a Scania diesel in 1961, and remained in the puffer trade – owned from 1974 by the Glenlight Shipping Company, an associated company of J. Hay. In 1980, she was withdrawn and laid up at Bowlingham, before being acquired in 1982 by the enthusiast group the West of Scotland Boat Museum Association. In 1983, she became a museum exhibit at the Scottish Maritime Museum, Irvine, North Ayrshire.

Vital Spark, (ex-*Eilean Eisdeal*, ex-*Elseda*, ex-*VIC 72*), was built by Brown's Shipyard, Hull, in 1944, and was sold out of naval service at Devonport Dockyard (where she had been a stores carrier) in 1968, and was then motorised and renamed *Elseda*, based at Troon as a cargo vessel. In 1972, she was purchased by Hugh Carmichael of Craignure, Isle of Mull, and worked around the islands dredging coal from sunken vessels. In 1984, she was purchased by Chris Nicholson of Easdale island, near Oban, and was renamed *Eilean Easdeal* to run an inter-island cargo service around the Western Isles until 1994. In 2001, she was brought to the Inveraray Maritime Museum, where she still is, and in 2006, she re-registered as *Vital Spark*, the name of the fictional puffer that appeared in the Para Handy books of Neil Munro. She has a Saab Scania 340-bhp diesel engine and still makes sailings.

Maggie (ex-*VIC 27*) was built by Pimblott in 1943 and was used as an Admiralty water carrier in the Liverpool area. She was later in service at Rosyth Dockyard (still as a water carrier) until being sold in 1966. Her new owners, Glenburn Shipping, Glasgow, intended to convert her to a yacht, but she was laid up at Ardrossan. In 1968, *VIC 27* was sold to Sir James Miller and converted at Granton for passenger use, with sleeping accommodation in her hold for up to twenty passengers; the crew still lived in their traditional accommodation in the bows of the vessel. She was renamed *Auld Reekie* in 1969 when she returned to steam and became a youth training vessel out of Oban, operated by the Land, Sea and Air Trust. In 1978, she was purchased by Bathgate Bros (Marine) Ltd and was used for charters. In 1994-95, she was used in the filming of the BBC television series based on Munro's books, bearing the name *Vital Spark* during this time (although not re-registered in this name). She was then laid up at Crinan in need of a new boiler. In 2006, she was purchased (in poor condition) by the owner of the Inveraray Maritime Museum and moved to Inveraray. She still has her original engine (built by Crabtree, of Great Yarmouth), and has been renamed *Maggie* after a fictional puffer that appeared in the film *The Maggie*. In November 2009, she was on the slip at Crinan Boatyard for major restoration work.

Small VIC Class:

Displacement: 124 tons. Gross registered tonnage: 96. Length: 66.85 feet (20.4 m). Beam: 18.5 feet (5.6 m). Draught: 8 feet (2.4 m).
Propulsion: steam two-cylinder reciprocating compound engine, 120 ihp, single screw. Single vertical coal-fired boiler.
Speed: 7 knots. Range: 700 miles. Bunkers: 11 tons.
Cargo capacity: 100 tons.
Crew: Two officers and four men.

Of the larger type, *VIC 56* – now at Chatham Historic Dockyard – was built by James Pollock & Sons Ltd, Faversham, in 1945 as an oil-burning steamer for carrying ammunition. Her boiler was of a convertible coal/oil-fired design. Like the other VICs, she had an open navigating platform – later, a wheelhouse was added by the Admiralty. Her early use is unclear, but by 1947, she was allocated to the Victualling Store Officer at Rosyth Dockyard. She spent thirty years at Rosyth, first as a stores carrier and later as an ammunition carrier, before being offered for sale in September 1978. In April 1961, she had sailed via the Caledonian Canal to the island of South Rona with construction materials to establish a base there. Her last recorded steaming with the Admiralty was in February 1975 and she was then laid up. After her sale for preservation, she sailed to the Thames in April/May 1979. *VIC 56* was then converted to coal-firing and the 2-ton capacity steel cargo derrick was replaced by a wooden one, which could be used to lower a boat by hand. Normally berthed at Anchor Wharf, Chatham Historic Dockyard, she is still in steaming condition.

  VIC 96 – now at Maryport, Cumbria – was built by Dunston in 1945 and still has her original Crabtree engine. She was based at Sheerness Dockyard until 1959, being renamed *C668* in April 1949. Following the closure of Sheerness Dockyard in 1959, she moved to Chatham Dockyard. In 1960, she was involved in a collision with the SS *Durango* and was repaired by Harland & Wolff, London. She was sold in 1972 to R. W. Fielding of Dublin, and was then berthed in the London Docks for some years. In 1981, she was purchased by the Maryport Maritime Museum and left the Limehouse basin to steam there via the Caledonian Canal. The museum sold her in 1986 to Allerdale District Council, by which point, she

Above: A close up of the superstructure on *Waverley*, seen in 2005, with her restored LNER livery. (Keith Belfield)

Below: Waverley in the Bristol Channel in 2006. (Chris Jones)

Kingswear Castle in service on the Medway in 2006. (Chris Jones)

Maid of the Loch in June 2006 on the slip for inspection, at Balloch on Loch Lomond where she is a café/bar/ restaurant ship and visitor attraction and is open daily between Easter and October and at weekends in winter. (Leslie Brown)

Above: The ornate, gilded sea serpent, which decorates the bow of *Gondola*. (Author)

Right: *Gondola*'s engine-room showing the boiler painted in Furness Railway maroon. (Author)

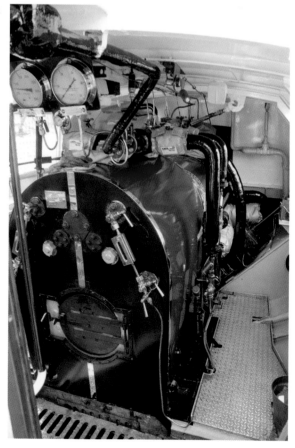

The elegant, upholstered first class saloon in *Gondola*, decorated with walnut trim. (Author)

At Bowness Pier, on Windermere, *Tern* prepares to embark passengers for Waterhead in April 2009, showing her distinctive canoe bow. (Author)

Following her conversion to diesel propulsion, *Tern* had a squat funnel in Sealink colours in this postcard view of her interim appearance.

Swan approaches Bowness, on Windermere, in April 2009, showing her latest appearance with funnels, an enclosed bridge, full-width main deck saloon and covered top deck. (Author)

Lady of the Lake in her most recent configuration as a motor vessel. She is seen approaching Howtown pier in April 2009. (Author)

Raven, as a motor vessel, underway between Patterdale and Howtown in April 2009. (Author)

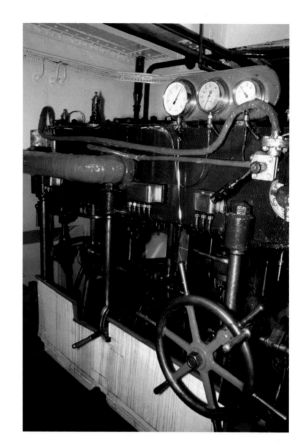

Right: Sir Walter Scott's steam engine. (Chris Allen)

Below: Sir Walter Scott steaming on Loch Katrine. This picture was taken before her 2008-09 refit. (George Lanyon)

Left: Manxman off Liverpool Pierhead during her operational service on the Isle of Man crossing. (Andrew King)

Below: Stern view of *Coronia* at Scarborough. (National Historic Ships)

Bow view of *Regal Lady* at Scarborough. (National Historic Ships)

Yarmouth Belle underway on the upper Thames. (Owner)

Karina on a cruise off the Isle of Man. (Steven Carter)

John H. Amos at Rochester on the barge *Narvik*, awaiting restoration, in June 2009. (Author)

The TID-class steam tug *Brent* at Maldon. (Martin Stevens)

The partially restored *Calshot* on display at Southampton in 2004. (Chris Jones)

The motor tug *Kent* alongside at Chatham. (National Historic Ships)

The motor tug *Wendy Ann* in 2009 in service at Ramsey in the Isle of Man. (Jenny Williamson)

Basuto and *Cuddington* at the Boat Museum, Ellesmere Port, in 2009

The VIC-class puffer *Spartan* at the Scottish Maritime Museum, Irvine, in 2008. (Johnny Durnan)

Left: *VIC 56*'s steam engine. (Chris Allen)

Below: The former fishing vessel *Blue Linnet* in Plymouth sound, 2006. (Gary Hicking)

Right: *Iveston* in No. 9 Dock at Portsmouth Dockyard, probably during the 1980s.

Below: The restored *MGB 81* at Bucklers Hard in 2007. (Author)

Above: The former Fairmile B class motor launch *Western Lady III* in service as an excursion vessel in 2005. (Steve Powell)

Left: The rescue and target towing launch *RTTL 2757* on display at the RAF Museum, Hendon, in 2002. (RAF Museum)

Right: VIC 56 steaming on the Thames in 1989. (Chris Allen)

Below: VIC 56 at Chatham Historic Dockyard's Anchor Wharf in 2006. (Author)

Left: *VIC 96*
seen as *C668*
at Limehouse
after her
sale by the
Admiralty.
(Martin
Stevens)

Below: *VIC
96* at
Maryport in
2003. (Martin
Stevens)

had reverted to *VIC 96*, and was sold for 50p to Giles Pattison ten years later. By this time, her condition had deteriorated to a critical point – on the condition that the vessel was preserved. Ownership subsequently passed to Martin Stevens of the Medway Maritime Trust. The *VIC 96* Trust was formed to restore the vessel at Maryport and intends to steam her to Chatham's No. 1 Basin where she will be based in seagoing condition.

Large VIC class:

Gross registered tonnage: 145. Length: 80.45 feet (24.5 m). Beam: 18 feet (5.5 m). Draught: 8.59 feet (2.6 m).
Propulsion: Steam compound engine, 140 ihp, single screw.
Cargo Capacity: 120 tons.
Crew: Two officers and four men.

FRESHSPRING

Between 1940 and 1946, fourteen steam-powered Fresh-class water tankers were built for the Admiralty by Lytham Shipbuilding & Engineering Co., Lytham St Annes, Lancashire. They were intended to carry fresh water to warships at dockyards and naval anchorages, and also had a limited fire-fighting and salvage capability. The last of the class to be built was *Freshspring*, laid down on 12 September 1945, launched 15 August 1946, and completed 10 February 1947. Her engines were manufactured by her builders. She became the sole survivor of the class.

Freshspring laid up, Gareloch, in the mid-1970s. (Michael Lennon)

Freshspring in 1992 at Collow Pill, Newnham on Severn, near Gloucester, where she is being restored. (Chris Allen)

    Freshspring was based at Malta in the fifties and early sixties, and then returned to the UK to operate on the Clyde and the west coast of Scotland with the Port Auxiliary Service. She was converted from coal to oil fuel in 1961. Surveyed and refitted at Ardrossan in 1969, she was then towed to Gareloch, where she remained until being offered for sale in 1977. *Freshspring* was sold on 4 July 1979 to a private owner, who towed her to Bristol, where she was adapted for the experimental use of alternative fuels to power ships' engines. Some time later, she was laid up at Newnham on Severn, Gloucester, and her condition deteriorated, but more recently, she was reportedly being gradually restored for youth, educational and pleasure purposes.

Displacement: 594 tons (885 tons full load). Gross Registered Tonnage: 282.9. Length: 126.25 feet (38.5 m). Beam: 24.5 feet (7.47 m). Draught: 10.8 feet (3.3 m). (12.5 feet full load (3.81 m)).
Propulsion: One triple-expansion steam reciprocating engine, 450 ihp, single Scotch boiler, single screw. Speed: 9.5 knots. Range: 500 nm at 8.5 knots. Bunkers: 46 tons coal.
Complement: 8-10.
Cargo capacity: 236 tons of water in six tanks.

KYLES

The veteran steam coaster *Kyles* was built on the Clyde in 1872 and traded until about 1982, by which time she was the oldest seagoing coaster trading under the Red Ensign. She retained the same name for all this time, despite having twenty-four changes of ownership and a number of conversions, which enabled her to serve successively as a general cargo vessel, sand suction dredger, salvage vessel, back to a general cargo vessel and, finally, a tanker. She is now on display afloat at the Scottish Maritime Museum, Renfrew.

Kyles was launched on 12 March 1872, by John Fullerton & Co., of Paisley, at their Merksworth yard, for Stuart Manford of Glasgow. Following the launching, the ship was taken to Glasgow, where her engines were fitted by their manufacturers, William King & Co. Of iron construction with pitch pine flush decks, she was equipped with a pitch-pine mast and derrick and a suit of sails. A single coal-fired boiler supplied the twin-cylinder steam engine. The first owner used her as a tender for the Firth of Clyde fishing fleet, bringing catches back to the rail-connected piers. In 1881, ownership passed to William Veitch, a chemical manufacturer at Crieff, and in 1886, the engine was converted to compound. Subsequent owners were in Newcastle, Hull, South Wales and Kent. Then, in 1926, her new owner in Cardiff converted her for sand suction dredging in the Bristol Channel area, and fitted a new boiler, which also served the steam-driven suction pump.

Between 1939 and 1942, she was laid up in poor condition before being sold to a salvage contractor and then, in 1944, to Ivor P. Langford, a ship owner and ship repairer based at Sharpness, near Gloucester. Langford – who was to own her

Kyles slipped for maintenance in 2008. (Johnny Durnan)

for thirty-seven years – converted *Kyles* back to a general cargo vessel, enlarging the forecastle and poop and adding improved and enlarged crew accommodation. The vessel worked in the Bristol Channel, and in 1953, a 120-bhp diesel engine (which dated from 1929) replaced the original steam engine. In 1960, she was converted into a sludge tanker, taking industrial effluents from Sharpness to be dumped in the Bristol Channel. In 1965, the engine was replaced by a Gardner diesel, and *Kyles* continued in service until 1974, when she became a sludge storage hulk. Then, in 1981, Langford sold her to Captain P. M. Herbert of Bude, Cornwall, who apparently put the ship back into trade.

On 8 November 1984, *Kyles* was purchased by the Scottish Maritime Museum to be placed on display at Irvine. In 1996, funding for a full restoration became available, and the ship was rebuilt to her 1953 motorised appearance. Work began in 1997 to strip out the sludge tanks, reinstate the original hatch and hatch cover, and replicate the mast and derrick. The wheelhouse had been removed in the 1970s and this was replicated from old photographs of the ship. In 1999, she undertook sea trials and became part of the Clyde-built exhibition at the museum's site on the Upper Clyde at Braehead, near Renfrew. Much of the hull is the original 1872 iron, whilst most of the upperworks date from major restorations in 1945 and 1998.

Gross tonnage: 122. Length: 77.1 feet (23.5 m). Beam: 18.2 feet (5.5 m). Draught: 8.1 feet (2.47 m).

RAVEN

The steam barge *Raven* was built in 1871 by Thomas B. Sneath & Co., Rutherglen, for the Furness Railway to provide cargo services in Lake Windermere. Her hull was of riveted iron, and her single-cylinder steam engine – which she still retains – was built by A. Campbell & Co., Glasgow. She had tiller steering and carried mail, coal, timber, farm produce, and general cargo from the Lakeside railway terminus to the houses and hotels beside the lake, especially those scattered on the western side, which lacked good road access, and the railway warehouses at Ambleside and Bowness. Before she was built, the only mode of transport around the lake was by laborious horse and cart over very poor roads. Her name derived from analogy with the Biblical ravens that fed Elijah when he was in the wilderness. It is said that the reward for carrying large quantities of beer on the ship was to tip the crew in kind and that this often resulted in a boathand being tied to the ship's crane on the return journey to prevent him falling overboard. During winter, *Raven* acted as an icebreaker for the Furness Railway passenger steamers.

Road competition brought her career to an end in 1922, and she was sold to Vickers Armstrong for testing mine-laying equipment. The present boiler was installed in about 1926. By the 1950s, *Raven* was abandoned and

Raven at the Windermere Steamboat Museum, Bowness, in 1980. (Author)

semi-derelict and, in 1956, was bought by George Pattinson, who amassed a collection of Windermere steam craft. In 1971, *Raven*'s engine and boiler were overhauled, and on her 100th birthday, she once again steamed down the lake, painted in her original Furness Railway colours. *Raven* and the other vessels in the collection were displayed in the Windermere Steamboat Museum, on the former sand and gravel wharf near Bowness, which opened in 1977. The museum closed in October 2006 for restoration, and passed to the Lakeland Arts Trust in 2007. *Raven* is the second oldest vessel on Lloyd's Register of Yachts and the oldest with her original engine. Her cargo hold has been converted into a saloon.

Gross tonnage: 41. Length: 71 feet (21.64 m). Beam: 14.5 feet (4.42 m). Draught: 4 feet (1.22 m).
Propulsion: single-cylinder steam engine, coal-fired boiler. Speed: 10 knots.

ROBIN

For over a century, steam coasters plied the inshore waters around the UK, linking ports large and small. When standing on any cliff top or headland, it was often possible to see several coasters steaming parallel with the coast in either direction, trailing smoke like the 'dirty British coaster with a salt-caked smoke-stack' of

Robin on display alongside West India Quay, London, in 2008. (Author)

Robin is being towed into St Katharine Docks after her partial restoration at Rochester, following her acquisition by the Maritime Trust. (Ambrose Greenway)

Masefield's poem. After the Second World War, they were gradually replaced by motor vessels, until the growth in size and numbers of lorries led to a steep decline in the number of coasters. Fortunately, there is one survivor – the *Robin* – which, for many years, could be seen at West India Quay, London, close to the Museum of Docklands.

Robin was built by Mackenzie, MacAlpine & Co. in Orchard House Yard, Bow Creek, in East London, who had received an order for two identical coasters from Robert Thomson, a London ship owner. The keels were laid in December 1889 and *Robin* was launched on 16 September 1890 (her sister ship *Rook* had been launched in the previous month.) Perhaps because of financial difficulties, ownership of the yard passed to Robert Thomson, under whose name the two ships were completed. *Robin* was fitted out in the East India Docks and moved in October to Dundee in Scotland to have her engine, boiler and auxiliary machinery fitted by Gourlay Bros. On her maiden voyage, which started from Liverpool on 20 December 1890, *Robin* steamed further than on any other voyage in the next ten years, reaching the port of Bayonne on France's Atlantic coast. She continued to trade around the south and west coasts of England, the Thames and Medway, and to France's channel coast. Her ownership in the first two years was complicated, as shares were transferred between various part-owners, but Arthur Ponsonby of Newport, Monmouthshire, was apparently the main owner. On 7 December 1892, *Robin* was sold to Alexander Blackwater to form the *Robin* Steamship Company: trading between Britain, Ireland and the continental ports, she carried cargoes including grain, iron ore, scrap steel, pit props, china clay, railway steel, general cargoes of casked and baled goods, and granite blocks for the Caledonian Canal. In her first decade of service, she visited 140 ports.

In May 1900, she was sold to Blanco Hermanos y Cia, of Bilbao, Spain, the beginning of seventy-four years under the Spanish flag, under the name *Maria*. Her ownership passed to Hijos de Angel Perez y Cia, of Santander, in 1913, and to Eduardo de la Sota Poveda, of Bilbao, in 1965. She traded around the Spanish coast with cargoes such as coal and scrap iron. During the First World War, she carried pig iron for the French government from the foundry at Santiago to Bayonne and Burdeos under French naval escort. Her appearance remained little changed for many years until, in a 1966 refit, her coal-fired boiler was converted to oil, the stern whaleback and the mizzen mast were taken out, the foremast, main mast and funnel were shortened, and the forecastle was extended.

In May 1974, she was purchased by the Maritime Trust and, in June, steamed under her own power to St Katharine Docks, London. She was restored at Rochester, renamed *Robin*, and opened to the public as part of the trust's collection of ships, which at that time were berthed in St Katharine Dock. In 1991, she moved to West India Quay and was subsequently bought by David and Nishani Kampfner, who set up a charitable trust. New restoration work began in March 2002, and she was equipped as an education centre with a large photographic gallery. In June 2008, a £1.9 million refit (funded by a loan from the Crossrail project) began at Lowestoft, following which she will return to London as a learning centre for disadvantaged children from the East End of London.

Gross registered tonnage: 366. Length: 143 feet (43.6 m). Beam: 22 feet (6.7 m). Draught: 13 feet (3.96 m).
Propulsion: three-cylinder triple-expansion steam engine, 60 ihp, single screw. Speed: 10 knots.
Complement: 12.

SHIELDHALL

A fine late example of a reciprocating steamer, *Shieldhall* was built for that most unglamorous of roles – dumping at sea the sludge (treated waste) from sewage works. One compensation for those aboard her was that for over twenty years she steamed out of the Clyde, amongst the beautiful scenery, to a point about four miles south of Garroch Head, the southernmost point of the Isle of Bute, passing *Waverley* and her consorts on their excursion routes. In fact, *Shieldhall* also carried passengers, free of charge to organised parties – including the underprivileged and senior citizens – in a long tradition of passenger carrying on Clyde sludge vessels.

She was laid down in October 1954, and launched on 7 July 1955, at the Renfrew yard of Lobnitz & Co. for Glasgow Corporation, and entered service on

Shieldhall on the River Dart in 2006. (Richard Walker)

20 October 1955. Lobnitz also built her two triple-expansion steam engines, and the boilers were built by Wm Simons & Co. Ltd of Renfrew. The engine-room was positioned aft and the bridge a little aft of amidships. The crew accommodation was in the raised forecastle, and the long main deckhouse contained officers' quarters and, for passengers, an observation lounge and a seventy-seat dining saloon. She served the sewage works at Shieldhall and, 4.5 miles downstream, Dalmuir, and then steamed 36.5 miles down the river and firth to the dumping grounds off Garroch Head, where discharge of her cargo was effected through large valves in the bottom of the sludge tanks. In May 1975, *Shieldhall* was taken over by Strathclyde Regional Council but was laid up in October 1976 at Port Glasgow, having been replaced by a new vessel.

In March 1977, she was purchased by Southern Water Authority for further service at Southampton. As part of an extensive refit, the passenger accommodation was converted into officers' accommodation and an owners' lounge, whilst the former officers' quarters right aft were converted into two-berth crew's cabins: the original crew's forecastle became a store. In November 1977, the ship steamed from the Clyde to Southampton, where she was to serve the sewage works at Slow Hill Copse, Millbrook and Woolston. She spent two and a half years in lay-up because the authority still had other vessels under contract, and did not enter service until 9 June 1980. Her dumping grounds were six miles south of the Nab Tower.

Shieldhall was withdrawn from service on 5 April 1985 and was purchased by the Solent Steam Packet Ltd in June 1988 for preservation in steaming condition. Her first voyage under preservation was on 9 June 1991. She has a grey hull, red boot-topping, white upperworks, and a buff funnel with a black top, and is based in Southampton Docks. Her passenger carrying certificate has been renewed, enabling her to operate seagoing excursions (from both Southampton and Weymouth) and charters, as well as being available alongside as a conference and function venue. She can now carry up to 150 passengers.

Gross registered tonnage: 1,792. Length: 268 feet (81.7 m). Beam: 44.7 feet (13.6 m). Draught: 13.3 feet (4.1 m).
Propulsion: two triple-expansion steam engines, 1,600 shp, twin screw. Two oil-fired Scotch boilers.
Speed: 13 knots. Bunkers: 78 tons of oil fuel.
Complement: 12. Passengers: 80 (as built).

CHAPTER 7
Service Vessels

BERTHA – DRAG BOAT

Believed to have been designed by Isambard Kingdom Brunel, the drag boat *Bertha* (this may originally have been a nickname) was built in about 1834 of riveted iron with a wooden superstructure. She is the oldest operational steam-driven vessel in Britain – and possibly the world – and has a coal-fired single-cylinder steam engine. The motion is transferred to the main drive shaft (which can be recognised by the large flywheel) by means of a single-reduction spur wheel drive. The vessel moves by hauling herself along a chain, the ends of which are attached to quayside bollards.

Rather than dredging mud out of the water, a drag boat drags silt from the edges of docks or under bridges by means of a flat blade on a boom, which is lowered by chains from the stern of the vessel. The silt is dragged into places where a current can remove it. Drag boats were out of date by the end of the Victorian era and had mostly been replaced by dredgers. Remarkably, *Bertha* continued and gave at least 120 years of service.

She was built by G. Lunnel & Co., Bristol, and was probably assembled in Bridgewater where she worked in the docks, firstly for the Great Western Railway and, after nationalisation in 1948, for British Railways. Her steam engine was also built by Lunnel, whilst her boiler was by Abbott, of Newark. Her working life ended in 1968, when the docks closed to commercial traffic. In 1970, *Bertha* was presented by British Rail to the Exeter Maritime Museum. After that museum closed in 1997, she moved with other parts of the collection to the Eyemouth Maritime Centre, Berwickshire, where she is exhibited in the World of Boats display.

Gross tonnage: 60. Length: 49.25 feet (15 m). Beam: 13.5 feet (4.11 m). Draught: 4 feet (1.22 m).
Propulsion: single-cylinder double-action engine, hauling chains.

EDMUND GARDNER – PILOT CUTTER

For nearly thirty years, *Edmund Gardner* and her two sister ships carried the pilots who guided the teeming stream of ships entering and leaving the River

Bertha in 1989 when at the Exeter Maritime Museum. (Chris Allen)

Bertha's steam engine. (Chris Allen)

Mersey. She was launched by Philip & Sons Ltd, Dartmouth, on 9 July 1953 for the Mersey Docks and Harbour Board, who were responsible for providing the Liverpool pilotage service, and she entered service in December of that year. Like her two sister ships, she was named after a former chairman of the board. They had diesel-electric propulsion and worked a rota of one week on station at the Mersey bar, one week at the outer station off Point Lynas, Anglesey, and one week either serving as a supply boat and tender to the other two cutters or under maintenance in the docks. If weather conditions were too bad to transfer pilots to ships, the cutters would themselves lead ships across the bar. They were considered to be particularly good ships in heavy weather and could remain on station in conditions up to Force 11. In addition to her crew, *Edmund Gardner* had accommodation for thirty-two pilots and eleven apprentice pilots.

In 1963, *Edmund Gardner* was involved in a collision with the ore carrier *Iron Horse* on the Mersey after the steering gear failed on the latter vessel. *Edmund Gardner* was hit on the starboard side, rolling heavily and damaging the bridge deck and hull plating – the repairs to the ship are still visible. The cutters were eventually replaced by high-speed launches, and in April 1981, *Edmund Gardner* was withdrawn from service. She was sold in 1982 to the Merseyside Maritime Museum and is now preserved in the Canning Graving Dock, Liverpool.

Gross tonnage: 701. Length: 177.4 feet (54.1 m). Beam: 31.7 feet (9.66 m). Draught: 10.16 feet (3.1 m).
Propulsion: two six-cylinder National diesel engines, 640 bhp, driving a generator for electric motor, single screw. Speed: 14 knots.
Crew: 11.

Edmund Gardner in the Canning Graving Dock, Liverpool, in 2009, during redevelopment of the site – when she was temporarily closed to the public. (Author)

EXPLORER – RESEARCH VESSEL

Explorer was launched on 21 June 1955 by Alexander Hall & Co. Ltd, Aberdeen, (who also built her triple-expansion engine) as a fisheries research ship for the Department of Agriculture & Fisheries for Scotland. Of riveted steel construction, she has the lines of a deep sea trawler. Trawling gear was fitted on the starboard side and heavy gallows and sheaves allowed the largest size of trawling gear of the time to be worked. Two electric hydrographic winches were fitted on the port side, while a steam plankton winch was fitted on the boat deck aft.

Her port of registry was Leith, but in service, she was based at Aberdeen's Torry Research Station. She worked in the traditional north-east Atlantic fishing grounds, as well as steaming further afield to Greenland, the Barents and White Seas north of Russia, and sometimes into the Arctic ice fields (for which her hull had been strengthened). Her work included monitoring both the main fish and shellfish stocks exploited by Scottish fishermen, and environmental changes to such things as current patterns and pollution levels. Research conducted aboard her contributed to the development of fish finders, new types of fishing gear, and modern net shapes, amongst other things.

After being taken out of service in 1984, she was sold to Jas A. White for scrapping at Inverkeithing. A reprieve came when she was acquired from the ship-breakers by Aberdeen City Council for preservation, but this project was aborted due to the lack of a suitable berth near the City Maritime Museum. In 1994, it was again proposed that she should be scrapped, but she was saved by the SS *Explorer* Preservation Society, formed by volunteers in February 1995 to restore her. She was moved to a berth at Leith, where conservation work continues, and tours of the vessel can be made by appointment.

Explorer on display in Leith Docks in 2005. (Chris Allen)

Gross tonnage: 831. Length: 201.9 feet (61.54 m). Beam: 32.7 feet (10 m).
Draught: 14.2 feet (4.32 m).
Propulsion: triple-expansion steam engine, 1,300 ihp, oil-fired Scotch boiler, single
screw. Speed: 12 knots. Range: approx. 8,000 miles. Bunkers: 267 tons fuel oil.
Crew: 38 (including 8 scientists).

JOHN ADAMS – TENDER

Built in 1934 by Richard Dunston Ltd, Thorne, for the Admiralty, *John Adams*
was named after a Secretary of State for Ireland. She was a motor cargo vessel
and was used as a tender at the Royal Dockyard, Haulbowline, Ireland. On
11 December 1938, she was handed over to the Irish Government at Cobh to
continue in service at Haulbowline dockyard, and remained in use there until
1987. The vessel is now at Bideford, Devon, where a restoration programme had
been started by Peter Herbert. Her original engine was a six-cylinder diesel (by
Mirrlees, Bickerton & Day, 125 bhp, speed 8 knots); she now has a larger diesel
engine (built in 1975, and probably fitted then).

Gross tonnage: 94. Length: 85.25 feet (26. m). Beam: 19.67 feet (6 m). Draught:
7 feet (2.13 m).
Propulsion: Mirrlees Blackstone diesel, 226 bhp, single screw. Speed: 10 knots.

John Adams at Bideford. (National Historic Ships)

A spectacular display by *Pyronaut*. (Bristol Industrial Museum)

PYRONAUT – FIRE FLOAT

This self-propelled fire float has been restored to full working order by the Bristol Museum Service and her spectacular displays of water spraying can be seen from time to time at events in harbour there. Built by Charles Hall & Sons Ltd, at their Albion Dock, Bristol, in 1934 as *Phoenix II* for Bristol City Council, she was used for fire-fighting in the city docks, allowing access to buildings and ships that were difficult to reach by land-based fire engines. She was also used at the Avonmouth Docks as they developed to supplant trade at Bristol. *Pyronaut* was particularly busy during the blitz of Bristol in the Second World War and was constantly manned throughout the worst raids.

Commissioned in June 1934, she was powered by Petter Atomic diesel engines and equipped with Merryweather three-cylinder reciprocating pumps, to work from Bristol's Prince Street Bridge river police station. In 1938, she was renamed *Pyronaut*. In 1968-69, the vessel was extensively refitted by Charles Hill, and a new Ruston & Hornsby diesel engine was installed together with Coventry Climax centrifugal pumps. However, declining trade in the docks led to her withdrawal in 1973, and she was sold to the Port of Bristol Authority for conversion into a diving boat to be used at Avonmouth. When this conversion was abandoned, *Pyronaut* was sold to a private owner, who reinstated her pumps and began to create a living space. In 1989, shortly before completing this work, he sold the vessel to Bristol City Museum & Art Gallery, who restored her completely. She is now based at the Prince's Wharf site of the new Museum of Bristol, berthed with the tugs *Mayflower* and *John King*.

Gross tonnage: 20. Length: 55 feet (16.8 m). Beam: 13 feet (4 m). Draught: 3 feet (0.9 m).
Propulsion: Ruston & Hornsby diesel engine.
Crew: 5.

VIGILANT – CUSTOMS CRUISER

Cox and Co., of Falmouth, completed *Vigilant* for the Commissioners of His Majesty's Customs in August 1902. As well as building the ship, they also manufactured her triple-expansion steam engine. She was to be based at Gravesend, providing Customs control to ships using the Port of London, but was designed to also cruise beyond the Thames Estuary, between Yarmouth and Dover. A panelled deckhouse on the afterdeck provided accommodation for senior officials and VIPs, effectively allowing her to double as a yacht for members of the Board of Customs, and in August 1903, *Vigilant* embarked on the first of her annual summer 'inspection' cruises, visiting every port between Gravesend and Penzance.

On 24 June 1911, *Vigilant* attended King George V's Coronation Review of the Fleet at Spithead, where, under a charter dating back to King Charles II, HM Customs & Excise (which had amalgamated in 1909) asserted their right for the ship to proceed down the lines of warships despite objections from the Admiralty. Dressed overall, she then anchored at the head of the line before the inspection of the fleet by the King in the Royal Yacht *Victoria and Albert*, which entered the

Vigilant arriving at Faversham prior to her restoration. (Martin Stevens)

lines to the thunder of a Royal Salute. Eighteen foreign and 165 British warships were present, including the flagship of the Commander-in-Chief Home Fleet, HMS *Dreadnought*. *Vigilant* is now the only surviving vessel from that review.

In 1920, she was sold out of the Customs & Excise service and was converted from steam to diesel to become the yacht *Shalimar*. She was laid up, under American ownership, during the Second World War, and continued cruising after the war. Renamed *Eileen Siocht*, she was bought by Mrs Nancy Kelly, who lived aboard her as a houseboat in Shoreham until 1988. She was sold with the berth to a property developer but came to the attention of the head of Customs Maritime Branch, who formed the *Vigilant* Trust to purchase and save the vessel. *Vigilant* underwent repairs to her hull at Vosper Thornycroft's Portchester yard, but the plans for further restoration were hampered by lack of funds and the ship was given a temporary berth at Pounds ship-breaking yard at Tipner, Portsmouth. Here, she languished and sank at her berth, until Pounds threatened to break the ship up. The Medway Maritime Trust came to the rescue in 2006, taking possession of the vessel, pumping her out and arranging for her to be towed to Faversham. The *Vigilant* Restoration Trust was formed to seek funding for a full restoration. It is intended to install a steam engine salvaged from the tug *TID 154*, which was found derelict in Cyprus.

Gross tonnage: 140. Length: 100 feet (30.48 m). Beam: 16 feet (4.88 m). Draught: 7.87 feet (2.4 m).
Propulsion (original): triple-expansion steam engine, 200 ihp, single screw. Speed: 11 knots.

Vigilant at Newcastle in 1904. (Martin Stevens' collection)

CHAPTER 8

Fishing Vessels

BARCADALE

Completed as the drifter *Ebenezer* by Herd & Mackenzie, Buckie, in 1939, this vessel was requisitioned by the Admiralty immediately after completion. Operated by her owners – Gardens, from Portlussie, Buckie – she served throughout the war as a tender, ferrying crew to and from warships at the anchorage in Scapa Flow. After the war, she entered the fishery with Gardens, who operated her out of Buckie. She was later sold to operate out of Wick and, finally, Peterhead (with the number PD45). Her present owner bought her in 1973 from Peterhead where she was lying neglected, and renamed her *Barcadale*. Between 1974 and 1979, she was converted into a yacht with major restoration work. She is based at Oban and cruises mainly on the west coast of Scotland.

Net tonnage: 31. Length: 60 feet (18.3 m). Beam: 17.5 feet (5.33 m). Draught: 7 feet (2.13 m).
Propulsion: Gardner diesel.

BLUE LINNET

Built as *Linnet* in 1938 by J. & G. Forbes, Sandhaven, this vessel was a herring drifter commissioned and owned by a co-operative of local fishermen headed by James Webster, with the Caledonian Fishing Company as sponsors. Her builder's certificate reveals that she was ketch-rigged and of carvel construction on oak frames. Her gross tonnage then was 47.58 and she was propelled by a National engine of 120 bhp. *Linnet* was registered in Banff with the number BF464 and drifted for herring off the east coast of Scotland, and at certain times of the year, she would use seine nets. In 1939, she was requisitioned by the Admiralty to perform many local duties between Fraserborough and Scapa Flow. James Webster continued to fish with her after the war and, in 1948, installed a new Gardner diesel, which is still in place. The Webster family progressively bought out the shares of the other co-owners, so that, by 1959, they had complete ownership.

Barcadale as she appears today. (Norman Smith)

Blue Linnet during her fishing days, seen some time after the Second World War. (Gary Hicking)

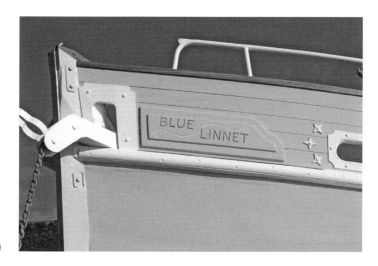

Bow detail on *Blue Linnet*. (Gary Hicking)

In 1962, *Linnet* was sold to Roy Middleton for conversion at Burnham-on-Crouch to a private yacht with nine berths. She was kept at Burnham-on-Crouch and later Salcombe, Devon, where she cruised local waters as well as making longer trips to France, Spain and the Mediterranean. In 1982, she was renamed *Blue Linnet*. In 1995, she was purchased by her present owners, Gary Hicking and his wife Anna Cattermole. Between 1995 and 1999, extensive work was carried out, with the help of professional shipwrights, to restore her to beautiful condition, and her owners have lived aboard since 1999. In 2003, *Blue Linnet* cruised all round the UK via the Caledonian Canal. She is now based in Falmouth, and her owners have plans to restore the gaff ketch rig.

Gross tonnage: 55. Length: 61.5 feet (18.75 m). Beam: 18 feet (5.5 m). Draught: 7.5 feet (2.3 m).
Propulsion: Gardner 6L3 diesel, single screw. Speed: 8 knots.

LYDIA EVA

Steam trawlers, fishing for sole, plaice, and other bottom feeding fish in the North Sea, were built in large numbers from 1881 onwards, replacing sailing trawlers, whilst steam drifters – which fished for herring and mackerel in shallower waters – did not eclipse the sailing drifters until the first decade of the twentieth century. In 1913, their peak year, 1,766 steam drifters fished out of Great Yarmouth and Lowestoft alone, together with only a handful of sailing drifters. The steam drifters continued to be seen in large numbers in East Coast ports until the Second World War, and one of them – *Lydia Eva* – was later rescued by the Maritime Trust for restoration.

The last vessel to be built by the Kings Lynn Slipway Co., *Lydia Eva* was a steam drifter/trawler ordered by Harry Eastick, a member of the Gorleston-on-Sea family, who owned and sailed drifters for over 120 years. The new vessel was named after the owner's daughter, and was larger and more powerful than a normal drifter, making her capable of following whichever line of fishing was the more profitable. Completed in July 1930, she fished for herrings for eight years, landing her last catch in December 1938 – by which time, the market for herring was severely depressed and the owner was losing money on his drifters. She was sold in 1939 to the Caernarvonshire Yacht Company, who converted her for a contract as a mooring vessel to service buoys for the Air Ministry's Bombing & Gunnery School at Abersoch, in mid-Wales. In 1942, she was requisitioned by the Ministry of War Transport for salvage work and, in 1947, was transferred to the Air Ministry as a mooring vessel and renamed *Watchmoor*. She subsequently saw service on stations at Ilfracombe, Maryport, Weymouth and Whitehaven, where she stayed until 1960. Then she passed into naval service at Pembroke Dock as part of the Port Auxiliary Service and, in 1966, the Marine Services Division. A new boiler and higher wheelhouse were fitted in the early sixties, but *Watchmoor* was laid up for sale at Milford Haven in 1969.

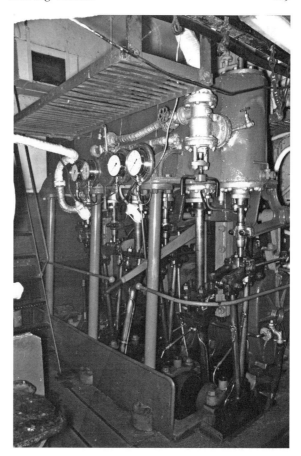

Right: The steam engine in *Lydia Eva*. (Chris Allen)

Below: Lydia Eva leaving Great Yarmouth on 9 August 1978 for St Katharine Docks. (Brian Ollington Photographers)

She was sold in 1971 to the Maritime Trust for preservation, restored to her original name and appearance, and, from 1973 to 1978, was on display at Great Yarmouth. From 1978 to 1986, *Lydia Eva* was part of the Maritime Trust's collection on display in St Katharine Docks, London. When that collection was dispersed in 1986, she was laid up in the West India Dock until 1990, when she was chartered to the *Lydia Eva* Trust and returned to the East Coast, at Lowestoft, to be opened to the public, both there and at Great Yarmouth. In 1995, she was sold for £1 to the *Lydia Eva* and *Mincarlo* Trust and remained on display until 2000, when a hull survey revealed that extensive underwater reconstruction was essential. Following a £839,000 grant from the Heritage Lottery Fund, an extensive restoration was started in March 2007 by Small & Co. at Lowestoft, and the ship returned to Great Yarmouth in May 2009.

Gross Registered Tonnage: 138. Length: 95 feet (28.96 m). Beam: 20.5 feet (6.25 m). Draught: 9.65 feet.
Propulsion: triple-expansion steam reciprocating engine, 41 rhp, single two-furnace Scotch boiler. Speed: 10 knots.

ROSS TIGER AND *ROSS LEOPARD*

These two Grimsby side-trawlers survive from the twelve Cat-class trawlers completed between 1957 and 1960 for the Ross Group. Built by Cochrane & Sons of Selby, *Ross Tiger* was the first of the class. At first, she was registered with Derwent Trawlers Ltd, a subsidiary of the Ross Group, and arrived at Grimsby in February 1957. She was re-registered in April 1963 with G. F. Sleight & Son, another Ross subsidiary, and again with Ross Trawlers in 1965. As a double-sided trawler, she was able to fish from either the port or starboard side, but her port-side gallows were removed in 1967, as the ability to work from both sides was no longer required. In 1969, her ownership changed to British United Trawlers. On each voyage, she spent three weeks fishing in the North Sea and off the coasts of the Faroes and Iceland, and packed up to 90 tons of cod and haddock in ice in her hold.

In the 1970s and early 1980s, the Cod Wars and their aftermath decimated the British deep-sea trawler fleet, and by 1984, the Cat-class trawlers were laid up in the Fish Docks at Grimsby. *Ross Tiger* landed her last catch around the middle of that year. On 25 January 1985, she was sold to Cam Shipping for use as an oil-rig support ship, and arrived in Lowestoft in June of that year for a conversion that stripped her of her trawling gear. The fishroom was converted into an accident recovery area and two davits were mounted on the port and starboard foredeck for the launching and recovery of two high-powered rescue launches. In order to facilitate their access to the ship whilst at sea, two apertures were cut into the gunwhales on the port and starboard sides. Sealed off by two doors, these 'rescue zones' were situated adjacent to the bridge, with another rescue zone a little

Ross Tiger at the Alexandra Dock, Grimsby, in 1994. (Chris Allen)

further aft. Another launch and davit were installed on the original boat deck. Renamed *Cam Tiger*, the vessel returned to Grimsby in October 1985 to serve her new owners.

In 1992, she was decommissioned and handed over to Grimsby Council for display at the National Fishing Heritage Centre as a tribute to the fishermen of the port. Equipment associated with her support ship role was removed, and between August 1992 and April 1993, she was reconverted to a trawler and the original name was reinstated. *Ross Tiger* opened to the public on 5 April 1993 and has remained so but is closed to the public during the winter.

Ross Leopard, the second of the class, was also built by Cochrane and was completed in October 1957. She also served as an oil-rig standby vessel between 1980 and 1991, renamed *Cam Leopard*. She was sold to her present owner in 1993 and, by 1995, had been converted to an art space and bar; her engine was removed to create space for a dance floor. Reverting to the name *Ross Leopard*, she has since been at various berths on the Thames.

Gross Tonnage: 326. Length: 130.8 feet (39.9 m). Beam: 26 feet (7.92 m). Draught: not known.
Propulsion: Ruston & Hornsby diesel engine, single screw.
Crew: 10-15.

CHAPTER 9
Yachts

CAROLA

Successful Victorian industrialists often flaunted their wealth through the ownership of elegant yachts, both sail and steam. One such is the steam yacht *Carola*, which was built in 1898 by Scott & Sons Shipbuilding & Engineering Co. at Bowling, on the Clyde, for the personal use of the Scott family, who owned her until 1959, when ownership passed to the company. The engine was manufactured by Ross & Duncan, Govan. She was of riveted steel construction with teak decks and superstructure and her accommodation included a saloon, owner's cabin, aft cabin and a small galley within the deckhouse. *Carola* carried the family on holiday cruises, including annual visits to the family's summer home at Colintraive on the Kyles of Bute. She also took groups of senior yard staff on Clyde cruises, whilst in the winter months, she served as a tender and tug.

During the Second World War, she was fitted with fire-fighting apparatus and a steam-driven fire pump to serve as a fire tender at the yard. In the 1950s, she broke away from her mooring on the River Leven and was blown ashore. Subsequently, she fell into a semi-derelict state and was sold in 1964 to Mr Manning of Glasgow, who kept her at Garelochhead and on the River Leven. He maintained the yacht until 1970, when Kenneth Gray, of Sway, Hants, bought her, and she was for a time berthed at Bucklers Hard on the Lymington River. In 1981, she was sold to a marine company called Plysosene, of Southwater, Sussex, and refitted for use as a promotional and corporate hospitality vessel. All of the public areas were renovated, a galley was installed in the owner's cabin, and the hull was repaired. A 50-bhp Thornycroft diesel auxiliary engine was installed to power new bow thrusters to give improved manoeuvrability. In 1990, ownership passed to Z-Guard Zinc Anodes Ltd, also of Southwater, Sussex. In 1992, the access flap to the boiler failed, filling the engine-room with steam and tragically killing two crewmen.

Later in the 1990s, *Carola* was acquired by the Scottish Maritime Museum and is displayed at Irvine. She now has a large saloon or fore cabin with teak skylight and teak saloon table. Her moulded oak panelling and brass gimballed light fittings are original, as are the seats on either side of the cabin. There is also an aft cabin with four bunks and a WC/shower. The original engine was restored,

Carola at Bucklers Hard in the 1980s.
(Author)

whilst the boiler – manufactured by Marshall & Anderson, Motherwell – dates from 1952. The funnel and hull are now painted in the original colours of cream and black respectively.

Gross tonnage: 40. Length: 70.4 feet (21.46 m). Beam: 13 feet (3.96 m). Draught: 7.4 feet (2.26 m).
Propulsion: two-cylinder compound steam engine, 80 ihp, single screw.

ESPERANCE

An earlier example of an industrialist's steam yacht is *Esperance*, now the oldest vessel on Lloyd's Register of Yachts. She was built in 1869 at Rutherglen by T. B. Sneath & Co. for Henry Schneider, who had made his fortune in iron ore and iron smelting on the Furness Peninsula and was a co-founder of the Furness Railway. *Esperance*'s iron hull was constructed with counter-sunk rivets to give a smooth finish to the outside of the hull. She is thought to have been the first twin-screw steam yacht. On completion, she was transported to Barrow-in-Furness and was then taken by train to Lakeside, on Windermere. The double railway track had to be specially singled under the bridges to let her through. Schneider moved to Belsfield House, above Bowness Bay, in 1869 and used his new yacht each day to

Esperance at the
Windermere Steamboat
Museum. (National Historic
Ships)

travel from Bowness to Lakeside, breakfasting as he went. He then boarded his
own private carriage on the Furness Railway steam train to Barrow, where his
office was.

By 1900, *Esperance* was owned by the Ferry Hotel, Bowness, and took visitors
to the hotel for afternoon teas. Hotel guests were also ferried up the lake for the
morning service at Wray Church. At some point, her steam engine was replaced by
a petrol engine. By the 1930s, the yacht had been converted into a houseboat and
was moored near Ramp Holme, on Windermere. She was apparently noticed by
the author Arthur Ransome and became the model for Captain Flint's houseboat
in his *Swallows and Amazons*; she was used as such by the BBC in their film
adaptation of the book. In 1941, *Esperance* sank in 20 feet of water but was
successfully salvaged by T. C. Pattinson. She later became part of the collection at
the Windermere Steamboat Museum, near Bowness, which opened in 1977 (the
museum is currently closed for renovation).

*Net tonnage: 15. Length: 65 feet (19.8 m). Beam: 10 feet (3.05 m). Draught: 4.5
feet (1.37 m).*
Propulsion: formerly steam, latterly petrol engine, twin screw.

UNDINE

The auxiliary steam yacht *Molly* was built in 1895 by Camper & Nicholsons, as a gentleman's yacht. She was sailed in the Solent area and also followed the J-class yacht regattas to other ports. Her hull is of carvel construction of pitch pine on oak with teak topsides on oak. She was requisitioned by the Admiralty in 1914 for harbour patrol duties and renamed *Undine*. After the war, she returned to use as a yacht (still named *Undine*) until being requisitioned again in the Second World War, when she was renamed *Watermaiden*. In 1945, she was returned to her owner, her wheelhouse was enlarged, and she reverted to the name *Undine*; in 1947, she was re-engined with an Atlantic diesel. In 1979, she became *Undine of Solent*, a name she retained until 1990, when her accommodation was restored by Tough's and she again became *Undine*. She retains the characteristics of a classic Victorian auxiliary yacht, is now based in London, and her present owner cruises her extensively in Scotland, the South Coast and France.

Net tonnage: 16. Length: 68 feet (20.73 m). Beam: 10.8 feet (3.3 m). Draught: 5.8 feet (1.77 m).
Propulsion (current): Gardner diesel engine, and sail.

Undine underway. (Owner)

CHAPTER 10

Naval Vessels

TON-CLASS COASTAL MINESWEEPERS

The Ton-class coastal minesweeper (CMS) was the most numerous class of British warship to be built since the Second World War, and one of the most successful. 117 were built for the Royal Navy and they remained in service for over forty years. The design was also adopted for new construction by the French, Dutch, Canadian and South African navies, and RN Tons were sold or transferred to seven Commonwealth and foreign navies. Now three of the class remain in UK waters: *Iveston* is a static sea cadet training ship at Tilbury, *Bronington* is laid up at Birkenhead, and *Wilton* is a yacht club headquarters ship at Leigh-on-Sea.

Although the Royal Navy had a large fleet of minesweepers that were built in the Second World War, it was decided in about 1947 that new classes should be built. In part, this recognised that mine technology was advancing, so that minesweepers had to deal with magnetic and acoustic mines as well as contact mines. Also, these mines were thought likely to be laid in shallow coastal and inshore waters in the approaches to ports and harbours. The main threat came from the Soviet Union who, it was estimated, could lay 4,500 – 6,000 mines per month in British waters. The Royal Navy's fleet of *Algerine*-class ocean minesweepers were designed to deal with deeply laid moored mines, whilst the smaller motor minesweepers were hastily built utility wartime designs with a limited life expectancy.

As a result, designs were produced in 1949 for a new coastal minesweeper and a new inshore minesweeper, as well as minehunter variants of each. Orders for the ships were expedited following the onset of the Korean War. The first batch of fifteen CMS was ordered on 9 September 1950 and the names were to be those of insects with colour adjectives as prefixes, such as *Green Beetle*, *Golden Ant* and *Blue Bee*. However, these names were soon deemed unsuitable, and in 1952, numbers were substituted, but were soon replaced by village names ending in 'ton'. The first of the class to be completed was *Bildeston* in April 1953, followed by *Coniston* in the following month. The coastal minehunter variant was to be the Thorpe class, and three were ordered but were cancelled in March 1953, mainly because of the lack of suitable minehunting sonar at the time. The inshore minesweepers and minehunters were built as the Ham and Ley classes respectively.

The general layout of the Ton class borrowed most heavily from the American BYMS of the Second World War, some 150 of which had served in the Royal Navy. They had been designed on warship lines, unlike the RN's motor minesweepers, which were based on commercial motor fishing vessel designs. The Tons were designed to have a minimal magnetic signature, so that they could sweep magnetic mines. Hence they were built of double mahogany hull planking on aluminium-alloy frames, with aluminium-alloy superstructure and non-magnetic fittings. The original ships had an open bridge, lattice mast, and a short funnel, and the underside was copper plated. The funnel was soon heightened so that exhaust fumes from the Mirrlees diesel engines were blown clear of the deck. The Mirrlees diesels were a stopgap before the more powerful Napier Deltic diesels became available; hence most of the early ships, such as *Bronington*, were re-engined, whilst *Highburton* and later ships were completed with Napier Deltics. On the afterdeck was an array of minesweeping gear including paravanes (floats) with davits, and winches designed to tow different sweeps for contact, acoustic and magnetic mines. A wire sweep was towed with explosive cutters to cut moored mines loose from their mooring cables, after which they were destroyed with gunfire. Influence sweeps were towed which could mimic the characteristics of larger ships and trigger the detonation of mines. Abaft of the funnel, a twin 20-mm Oerlikon anti-aircraft gun was mounted, whilst on the foredeck was a single 40-mm Bofors anti-aircraft gun. The copper hull sheathing was later replaced by Cascover nylon.

In the light of the Cold War threat, there was a requirement for a large number of the new minesweepers, and by May 1954, it was planned to build 167 coastal minesweepers and 167 inshore minesweepers (IMS). In fact, 116 CMS and 101 IMS were built in British yards, even though it was always envisaged that many of them would be laid up in reserve. In the event of hostilities, it was planned that the reserve ships would be manned by reservist (RNR and RNVR) personnel, the latter being trained in minesweeping during peacetime through the attachment of Ton-class ships to their units. The construction of the Tons was shared by sixteen different shipbuilders, many of them small yards. John I. Thornycroft at Southampton acted as the parent firm, building the lead ship, *Coniston*, and several others, and acting as an adviser to the smaller firms.

The first operational group of eight Tons, the 104th Minesweeping Squadron, was formed in 1954, and by 1956, there were two squadrons in the Mediterranean and two in home waters. A further twelve vessels were attached to Royal Naval Volunteer Reserve divisions as seagoing tenders, taking division-specific names such as *Humber*, *Curzon* and *Killiekrankie*. As greater numbers emerged from their builders' yards, many were cocooned in reserve, the largest concentration being at Hythe on Southampton Water, where HMS *Diligence* was a shore base for commissioning and equipping the new minesweepers between 1953 and 1960.

When suitable sonar became available, *Shoulton* was converted in 1957 to a prototype minehunter for trials purposes. Building on this experience, *Kirkliston* was converted in 1964 to become the first operational minehunter and a further thirteen conversions followed. They were fitted with an enclosed bridge, tripod mast, and new radar, and minehunting sonar was installed on the underside of the hull beneath the bridge, to detect mines ahead of the ship. Active rudders were fitted to allow the minehunter to position over the mine, and four divers and two inflatable dinghies were carried to permit the mine to be disposed of safely, either by laying explosive charges or bringing them inboard and defusing them. The twin 20-mm gun was removed, as was some of the minesweeping gear.

The Tons saw service around the world. For example, in 1965, there were squadrons based overseas at Malta, Singapore, Hong Kong, and Bahrain, and in home waters at Port Edgar, Portsmouth and Portland, plus the Fishery Protection Squadron and the Royal Naval Reserve Squadron. An extra (second) squadron based at Singapore was commissioned during the period of confrontation with Indonesia, when the Ton class (two of which were manned by the Royal New Zealand Navy) played a leading role in intercepting incursions into Malaya and Borneo and were fired on by Indonesian forces.

Other units of the class were later to be involved in patrols against illegal arms shipments into Northern Ireland. In 1974, three of the class helped clear mines in the Middle East following the Egyptian-Israeli peace settlement, and ten years later, five of the ships were part of a multinational force clearing mines in the Gulf of Suez and the Red Sea. These mines had been laid by an unknown source and had damaged twenty ships before countermeasures could be taken. In the Royal Navy, five ships were converted to patrol craft, based at Hong Kong, and two to survey ships.

Forty years of active service of the Ton class in the Royal Navy came to an end in 1994, when *Nurton* and *Wilton* paid off. *Wilton* was an extra ship, the one 117th of the class, and was built of glass-fibre-reinforced plastic, testing the material that would be used in the later Hunt-class minehunters. *Wilton* was commissioned in 1973 – thirteen years after the last of the wooden ships, *Lewiston*, had entered service.

The survivors in the UK are:

BRONINGTON

Bronington was built by Cook, Welton & Gemmell at Beverley in Yorkshire and laid down on 30 May 1951. She was launched on 19 March 1953 by Mrs W. G. John, wife of the director, Naval Constructors, and completed on 4 June 1954. *Bronington* was named after a village near Wrexham. Built on the River Hull, a tributary of the River Humber, she was to remain in that area for four years. She entered service with the Royal Naval Volunteer Reserve's Humber Division and was renamed *Humber* in accordance with the custom at that time of RNVR divisions retaining a name for their allocated ship. She was part of the 101st Minesweeping Squadron, which comprised the various RNVR minesweepers

Bronington at Portsmouth in 1958, showing her original appearance, equipped as a minesweeper and with a twin 20-mm Oerlikon gun abaft the funnel. (World Ship Society)

Bronington at Birkenhead in April 2006, at the berth where she had been open to the public, shortly after the trust owning her went into liquidation. (Author)

Bronington seen in service after her conversion to a minehunter.

from ports around the coast of the British Isles (in 1958, the separate RNVR identity was lost through merger with the Royal Naval Reserve). Her crew was thus weekend sailors, and she was based at Hull for weekend training activities, whilst in the summer, she took part in cruises further afield with other units of her squadron. During this period, she won the Thornycroft Trophy for minesweeping excellence, against competition from both regular and reserve units. In 1958, the Humber Division was disbanded and she reverted to the name *Bronington* and joined the 100th Minesweeper Squadron, later the 1st Minehunter Squadron, at Port Edgar, near Rosyth on the Firth of Forth.

Between 1963 and 1965, *Bronington* was converted to a minehunter in Rosyth Dockyard. In February 1965, she recommissioned as part of the 5th Minesweeper Squadron, which was based at HMS *Vernon* in Portsmouth. She returned to Port Edgar to join the 1st Mine Countermeasures Squadron on 5 January 1966. On 15 February 1974, she sailed from Port Edgar to Gibraltar Dockyard for a major refit, and then returned to the Forth in 1976 for further service in home waters.

On 9 February 1976, HRH Lt the Prince of Wales took command for ten months, leaving the ship on 15 December 1976, his last day of active service after five years in the Royal Navy. On 14 November of that year, during a visit to the Pool of London, HMS *Bronington* was visited by the Queen, the Queen Mother, HRH Prince Philip and eight other members of the royal family. They toured the ship form stem to stern, stopping to chat with all the crew members.

From 1980, *Bronington* was part of the 2nd Mine Countermeasures Squadron, and was deployed to the Mediterranean, spending the last five months of 1983 detached in the NATO Standing Naval Force Channel, and was employed for a time in the Fishery Protection Squadron. During 1987, she spent some months refitting in Portsmouth Dockyard. Finally, she entered Portsmouth Harbour to pay off on 30 June 1988 after more than thirty years service.

In January 1989, *Bronington* was purchased by the *Bronington* Trust, a charity dedicated to her preservation and display, and on 24 January, she left Portsmouth for Manchester. She was opened to the public at Salford Quays on 28 October 1992. In mid-2002, ownership passed to the Warship Preservation Trust and she moved to Birkenhead on 11 July 2002. Here, she joined the frigate *Plymouth* and submarine *Onyx* on display until the trust was put into receivership and the ships were closed to the public on 5 February 2006. She has remained at Birkenhead (December 2009), whilst a new owner is sought, but her condition has seriously deteriorated and she may have to be scrapped.

IVESTON

Iveston was built by Philip & Son, Dartmouth, launched 1 June 1954 and completed 29 June 1955. She was named after a village near Consett, County Durham. After acceptance trials, she was placed in reserve at Hythe, on Southampton Water, until January 1963 when she was towed to Devonport for conversion to a minehunter, which was completed in October 1964. She then served in home waters in the 1st Mine Countermeasures Squadron, and – from 1972 – the 2nd Mine Countermeasures Squadron. In 1970, *Iveston* was the scene

Iveston leaving Portsmouth in 1968. (Author)

Iveston at Tilbury in 2009, serving as a static Sea Cadet headquarters ship. (Author)

of the last mutiny in the Royal Navy, while at anchor at Ullapool. Five drunken ratings refused duty sang rebel Irish songs outside the wardroom, and imitated characters from the film *Mutiny on the Bounty*. They were subsequently court-martialled, found guilty, and were jailed and dismissed from the service. On 29 July 1975, *Iveston* rescued the pilot of a twin-engined aircraft, which had ditched five miles south of the Isle of Wight. On 28 June 1977, the ship attended the Silver Jubilee Review of the Fleet at Spithead.

After paying off in 1992, she was transferred to the Thurrock Sea Cadet Corps unit and was towed to Tilbury Docks in August 1993 to become a static sea cadet training ship. The winch on the afterdeck was removed to accommodate a Portakabin-type training room. In 1999, she was purchased by the unit from the Ministry of Defence. Because she is berthed inside the docks, she cannot be seen without a special arrangement.

WILTON

Wilton was ordered on 11 February 1970 from Vosper Thornycroft, Woolston, and launched on 18 January 1972. She was named after a town in Wiltshire. Much of her equipment was taken from the Ton-class minesweeper *Derriton*, and was fitted after reconditioning, but new Napier Deltic engines were provided. She was completed on 12 June 1973 and was the first warship of this size to have a

Wilton leaving Portsmouth at some time in the early 1980s. (Michael Lennon)

Wilton photographed in 2009 at Leigh-on-Sea, where she is a clubhouse for the Essex Yacht Club. A 40-mm Bofors gun is mounted on the forecastle. (Author)

GRP (glass-fibre-reinforced plastic) hull. On 25 April 1973, she joined the 2nd Mine Countermeasures Squadron based at HMS *Vernon*, Portsmouth. *Wilton* served on mine clearance operations in the Middle East during 1974 and 1984; most of her other service was in home waters. Between January and June1977, and May 1979 to January 1980, she was part of the NATO Standing Naval Force in the Channel. On 28 June 1977, she was at the Silver Jubilee Review of the Fleet at Spithead.

In 1991, she was converted into a navigation training ship at Rosyth for service with the Britannia Royal Naval College, Dartmouth. She paid off at Portsmouth on 26 July 1994 and was laid up in Fareham Creek. *Wilton* was sold in August 2001 and towed to Southampton. In the following month, she was moved to Gillingham for conversion into a headquarters ship for the Essex Yacht Club, Leigh-on-Sea. She eventually arrived there in September 2004. Her funnel has been removed and windows have been cut into the hull side aft. Additional accommodation structures have been constructed on the after and foredecks, but a 40-mm Bofors gun is still mounted on the forecastle.

Elsewhere, one Ton survives as a museum ship: *Durban*, built by Camper & Nicholsons, Gosport, for the South African Navy, was launched on 12 June 1957. She left Portsmouth on 12 May 1958 and arrived at Simon's Town on 13 June 1958. She paid off on 23 October 1985 and was placed on display at the Port Natal Maritime Museum, Durban, South Africa.

Displacement: 360 tons (425 tons full load). Length: 152 feet (46.33 m). Beam: 28.75 feet (8.76 m). Draught: 8.2 feet (2.5 m).
Propulsion: two Mirrlees diesel engines, 2,500 bhp, later replaced by two Napier Deltic diesel engines, 300 bhp; two shafts. Speed: 15 knots. Range: 2,300 nautical miles at 13 knots.
Armament: one 40-mm Bofors anti-aircraft gun, two 20-mm Oerlikon anti-aircraft guns. The latter were removed on conversion to minehunter.
Complement: 29, increased to 38 as minehunter.

MTB 102 – MOTOR TORPEDO BOAT

In 1937, Vosper, at Portsmouth, built an experimental motor torpedo boat (MTB) of 68 feet in length as a speculative venture. When fully armed and loaded, she achieved 44 knots, and proved her seaworthiness in winds of Force 7. This impressive performance led to her being purchased by the Admiralty as *MTB 102*, and signalled the start of an extensive programme of MTB development and construction by Vosper during the Second World War – in which the Admiralty ordered 119 'short' Vosper MTBs ('short' implying a length of 70-73 feet.)

MTB 102 was launched in May 1937 and commissioned into the Royal Navy on 26 May 1938. Her petrol engines were built by Isotta-Fraschini, of Milan, Italy, and developed over twice the power of the Napier Lion engines used in pre-war MTBs.

MTB 102 on trials in February 1938, whilst still owned by the builders, showing the centreline bow torpedo tube port and the framework for launching torpedoes over the stern. (Vosper)

A 1938 view of *MTB 102*, now in commission with the Royal Navy, showing side-launching torpedo tubes and an Oerlikon gun mounted aft of the wheelhouse. (*MTB 102* Trust)

The crew of *MTB 102* in 1940, with Lt James (third from left in back row) in place of her normal commanding officer, twenty-one-year-old Lt Chris Dreyer. (*MTB 102* Trust)

The restored *MTB 102* in No. 2 Basin at Portsmouth Dockyard in 2005 for the International Festival of the Sea. (Author)

Originally, *MTB 102* was fitted with a single torpedo tube in her bow, which was subsequently supplemented by a frame for stern launching a second torpedo, but following trials, this combination was replaced by two 21-inch tubes on the side-decks. In early 1938, she carried a trial 20-mm Oerlikon gun, abaft the superstructure, and later (after her return from the Dunkirk operation) a twin 0.5-inch machine-gun was mounted in this position. In 1941, light 0.303-inch machine-guns were added, mounted forward on stanchions.

Once commissioned, she was attached to HMS *Vernon* at Portsmouth for further prototype torpedo launching trials. In March 1940, *MTB 102* was being used at HMS *Hornet*, Gosport, in the 3rd MTB (Training) Flotilla, providing basic sea training for the early intakes of coastal forces personnel. On 26 May 1940, *MTB 102* received orders to proceed to Dover at all speed. At this time, she had no gun mounted, so four Vickers 0.303-inch machine-guns were hastily fitted. After arriving at Dover at 7 a.m. on 27 May, the boat was ordered to Dunkirk, and during the evacuation of the British Expeditionary Force, *MTB 102* crossed the Channel eight times. She towed boats packed with soldiers off the beach to destroyers and other ships lying offshore, rescuing several hundred from the coast towards La Panne. When the destroyer *Keith* was bombed by a Stuka, Rear Admiral Wake-Walker, in command of naval operations, and his staff officers and two wounded crew members, were transferred to *MTB 102*. Wake-Walker used her as his flagship for the last two nights of the operation, directing the incoming and outgoing vessels at Dunkirk from the bridge. A rear admiral's flag was improvised from a dishcloth and red paint, and *MTB 102* was the third to last vessel to leave the scene when, on 4 June, the admiral directed the last of the evacuation from the bridge of the boat.

By late 1942, she was obsolete as an MTB and, on 21 January 1943, was transferred to the Royal Army Service Corps (RASC) and renamed *Vimy*. She was based at the Gunwharf, Portsmouth, and used for target towing. In 1944, she carried Winston Churchill and General Eisenhower on their review of the ships assembled on the South Coast in preparation for the D-Day landings. She was returned to the Royal Navy at Poole on 14 March 1945 and laid up in reserve. In 1948, she was sold to become a motor cruiser on the East Coast. Then, in 1973, whilst under conversion to a houseboat, she was acquired by the Blofield and Brundall Sea Scouts at Lowestoft and converted into a headquarters ship. Luckily, she was to find a role in the 1976 film *The Eagle Has Landed* for which she underwent restoration to full seagoing state, before being returned to the scout group. The hull and decks received further repairs and reinforcement in 1983 and 1990. She has been re-engined four times, in each case with diesel engines, the latest (two Cummins 600-bhp units) being fitted in 2002. In April 1996, she was handed over to the *MTB 102* trust and is now based at Lowestoft, but frequently attends maritime heritage and similar events at other ports during the summer.

Displacement: 32 tons (loaded). Length: 68 feet (20.73 m. 69.5 feet including trailing rudders). Beam: 14.75 feet (4.5 m). Draught: 3.25 feet (1 m).
Machinery (original): three-shaft, Isotta-Fraschini petrol motors, 3,450 bhp. Speed: 43.75 knots.
Armament: one 20-mm gun (later varied), two 21-inch torpedo tubes.
Bunkers: 990 gallons of petrol. Range: 240 nm at 35 knots, 1,100 nm at 9 knots.
Complement: 10 (2 officers and eight ratings).
Pennant Number: 102.

MTB 71 – MOTOR TORPEDO BOAT

MTB 71 was ordered by the Royal Norwegian Navy as their *MTB 7*, the keel having been laid down by Vosper at Portsmouth on 28 July 1939, but following the outbreak of war in September, she was requisitioned by the Admiralty. She was a 60-foot boat, armed with two 18-inch torpedoes and twin machine-guns, and had Isotta-Fraschini engines – giving a top speed of 39 knots. Completed on 2 July 1940, she joined the 11th MTB Flotilla at HMS *Wasp*, Dover. The flotilla's work included night-time anti- E-boat patrols and crash-boat duties (picking up 'ditched' fighter pilots and survivors from merchant ships sunk by the enemy). Two months later, during a heavy air attack on Dover, she was damaged, including a fire in her wheelhouse, and repairs at Whitstable took four months. In June

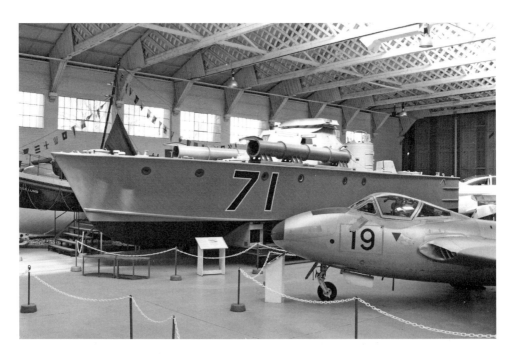

MTB 71 on display at Duxford in 2006. (Author)

1941, she was slightly damaged in action with enemy escort vessels off Etaples and her petty officer stoker was killed. The next month, in further action off Berck buoy, she was holed below the waterline and was out of action for two months whilst under repair on the Thames.

In November 1941, she re-commissioned with a Royal Norwegian Navy crew – to join the 1st MTB Flotilla at HMS *Beehive*, Felixstowe – and had a skirmish with E-boats off Kwinte Bank. In February 1942, she reverted to an RN crew and was involved in the Dover Straits, searching for the German *Scharnhorst*, *Gneisenau* and *Prinz Eugen* during their daring Channel dash on 12 February. *MTB 71* was recorded as being damaged that day by shellfire and was then under repair at Brightlingsea for six months. In September 1942, she transferred to the 4th MTB Flotilla at Felixstowe and was in action off the Hook of Holland two months later.

In June 1943, she was transferred to the Royal Army Service Corps and was laid up at Portsmouth and cannibalised for spares for her sister ship *MTB 72*, which had also been taken over by the army. Then, in September 1944, she was returned to the navy at HMS *Hornet*, and sold the following year for use as a houseboat, *Wild Chorus*, at Birdham. Her owner, Mr Pudney, died in 1992 and she was acquired by Hampshire County Council in conjunction with the *MTB 71* Group Charitable Trust. She underwent partial restoration within Portsmouth Dockyard before being moved to the British Military Powerboat Trust's yard at Marchwood for further restoration as a static exhibit. In April 2005, she was taken to the Imperial War Museum's site at Duxford, Cambridgeshire, where she is displayed in a hangar.

Displacement: 25 tons. Length: 60 feet (18.3 m). Beam: 15 feet (4.6 m). Draught: 3.5 feet (1.1 m).
Machinery: two Isotta-Fraschini V-12 petrol motors, 2,200 bhp, two shafts. Speed: 35 knots.
Armament: two 0.5-inch machine-guns, two 18-inch torpedo tubes.
Complement: 10 (2 officers and 8 men).
Pennant Number: 71.

MGB 81 – MOTOR GUNBOAT

During the Second World War, the British Power Boat Company (BPB) at Hythe, on Southampton Water, became a prolific builder of fast coastal forces craft for the Royal Navy. At first, they concentrated on motor anti-submarine boats and motor gunboats (MGB) and one of the latter, *MGB 81*, has survived and been restored to seagoing condition. Her design was produced by BPB in collaboration with the Admiralty and, in all, 105 of her type were built (including some which were completed as motor torpedo boats).

MGB 81 had a hard chine hull form using double-diagonal mahogany sides and a triple diagonal mahogany bottom. She had a hogged sheer deck and a streamlined superstructure, which contained the wheelhouse, bridge, chartroom and wireless office. Her three Packard 1,250-bhp petrol engines were manufactured in Detroit. Although ordered on 27 November 1940, *MGB 81* was not laid down until 16 December 1941. She was launched on 26 June 1942 and was by then virtually complete, for she was on trials by 8 July and achieved a speed of 38.63 knots on Southampton Water. Later, following the fitting of underwater exhausts, a speed of 43.43 knots was recorded.

She was accepted and commissioned on 11 July 1942 and then worked up at HMS *Bee*, the coastal forces base at Weymouth, before joining the 8th MGB Flotilla at Dartmouth in August 1942. Between then and September 1943, *MGB 81* was involved in six actions. Off Guernsey on the night of 13/14 August 1942, she engaged in a close-range gun attack on two enemy armed trawlers and one trawler was severely damaged. The next month, the flotilla moved to Felixstowe, and *MGB 81* was soon in action off the Hook of Holland on 14/15 September, when two enemy motor vessels were damaged by gunfire and four armed trawlers were hit, with no damage to the MGBs. In another action off Holland on 2/3 October, four enemy armed trawlers were engaged, and one of the flotilla, *MGB 78*, was lost. On 27/28 February 1943, the MGBs fought the escorts of a German convoy off the Hook, resulting in the sinking of *MGB 79*, and damage to *MGB 81* caused by a shell hitting the engine-room. In April 1943, the flotilla returned to Dartmouth, though *MGB 81* was refitting at Brightlingsea from 29 April to 20 May. In June 1943, she was damaged in collision with *MGB 115* and was repaired by BPB at Poole. On 11-12 September, she again sustained damage when fired on by shore batteries at Cap la Hague and spent the rest of the month being repaired at BPB's Poole yard.

In late September 1943, the boat was renumbered *MTB 416* and her designated armament was increased to reflect her new role, with the addition of two 18-inch torpedo tubes. Even though they were given the motor torpedo boat (MTB) classification, some of the former MGBs did not ship torpedo tubes, so it is not certain that *MTB 416* was so fitted. Her flotilla became the 1st MTB Flotilla and was redeployed to Ramsgate for a short period in October 1943 before returning to Dartmouth. *MTB 416* was refitted at Poole by BPB between 5 January and 2 March 1944. Her first recorded action as an MTB was in Lyme Bay on 21-22 April, when she engaged German E-boats and sustained action damage. Repairs were again made at Poole, but she was back in action for the Normandy landings, where she was involved from 6 to 30 June 1944, with Gosport as her base. On the night of 23/24 June, she was involved in an attack on a German convoy leaving Cherbourg. Although *MTB 416* was only backing up this operation, one of her crew was killed. On the night of 18/19 July, she obtained hits on German R-boats off Cap d'Antifer, but her hull was damaged by gunfire and she returned to Poole again for repairs. In September 1944, the flotilla's base changed to Lowestoft and her next action was on 14 February 1945 at Ostend.

On 27 April 1945, with the war in Europe in its final days, she paid off at Poole and was placed in reserve. On 2 October 1945, *MTB 416* was approved for disposal and was later sold. Little is known about her subsequent history until 1958, when she was arrested by Customs officers at Shoreham whilst on a smuggling operation. She was sold by the Admiralty Marshal to a Gosport scrap dealer, who removed her engines and running gear. She was sold on for use as a sailing school accommodation ship at Hardway, Gosport, and renamed *Jolly Roger*. In 1964, she was sold to become the houseboat *Cresta*, also at Hardway. In 1984, she was towed to Bursledon on the River Hamble, and in 1988, was bought by Guy Webster to restore her to her wartime appearance. On 17 September 1998, she was bought by Philip Clabburn and was reconstructed at the British Military Powerboat Trust's Marchwood site between 1999 and 2002. Petrol engines were thought to be prohibitively expensive to run, so three 1,000-bhp V-12 MAN turbocharged diesel engines were fitted, giving an estimated top speed of 45 knots. Since late 2009, *MGB 81* has been based at Portsmouth, following her acquisition by the Portsmouth Naval Base Property Trust.

Displacement: 46.6 tons. Length: 71.5 feet (21.8 m). Beam: 20.5 feet (6.2 m). Draught: 5.75 feet (1.75 m).
Machinery (original): three shafts, Packard petrol motors, 3,750 bhp. Speed: 40 knots.
Bunkers: 2,733 gallons of petrol. Range: 475 miles at 35 knots, or 600 miles at 15 knots.
Armament: one 2-pounder AA gun, two 20-mm AA guns, two 0.303-inch machine-guns, two depth charges. (two 18-inch torpedo tubes added as MTB 416).
Complement: 12.
Pennant numbers: 81 (to 1943), 416.

MTB 416 (formerly MGB 81), nearest the camera, together with MTB 413 and MTB 414, returning after dawn from an anti-E-boat patrol off Cherbourg in June 1944, as part of Operation *Overlord* (the Normandy Landings). (IWM neg. no. A24047)

RML 511 was a typical Fairmile B-class rescue motor launch, and is seen at Newhaven during the Second World War. In 1946, she was sold to become the excursion vessel *River Lady* on the River Orwell, but later became part of the Western Lady Ferry Service fleet in Torbay, retaining her name and serving until 1973. She then became a diving support vessel at Plymouth, but her ultimate fate is unknown.

Looking back towards Torquay from *Western Lady IV*. (Steve Powell)

FAIRMILE B-CLASS MOTOR LAUNCHES

At the outbreak of the Second World War, the Royal Navy recognised it had a need for large numbers of small craft for coastal escort and patrol work. The Fairmile company had anticipated this with the design of their 110-foot A-class motor launch, which had a hard chine hull and three Hall Scott Defender petrol engines (supplied on lease/lend from the United States of America). The first craft was ordered in July 1939 and eleven more were ordered in September of that year, shortly after war had been declared. Their wooden construction employed prefabricated parts using many subcontractors, mainly furniture makers. The frames were bonded plywood with double-diagonal mahogany planking, with double-skinned teak decks, and assembly was carried out by yacht-building yards. However, the A class had a limited range and were poor sea boats. The Admiralty's naval constructor, William Holt, produced a round chine design with only two Hall Scott engines and handed this to Fairmile to adapt to their building procedures: thus the very successful Fairmile B class was born. 388 were built in the UK and a further 266 in Egypt and Commonwealth countries. They became maids of all work, with numerous duties including convoy escort, anti-invasion patrols, ferrying troops, minesweeping, guiding landing craft onto beaches, ambulance launches, and air/sea rescue. For the last named role, fifty-two were completed as rescue motor launches (RML). In their various roles, the Fairmile Bs had a variety of armament – light guns, depth charges and even torpedo tubes. In RML guise, the armament consisted of one 2-pounder, one 20-mm and four 0.303-inch guns, plus six depth charges.

When the war ended, many of the Fairmiles were declared for disposal. Four of the RMLs were purchased by Ron Edhouse and Son in 1946-47 to form the Western Lady Ferry service to operate in Torbay, and a fifth was acquired in 1949. The RMLs were probably chosen because they had a sick bay deckhouse aft, which could serve as an undercover deck saloon for passenger service. Diesel engines were installed to replace the original petrol engines. Two of these vessels, *Western Lady III and Western Lady IV*, continued in service in Torbay until 2006. They had distinctive pale blue hulls, white upperworks, and red funnels with a black cap and white band. In 1963, ownership of the Western Lady Ferry Service had passed to Torbay Boat Construction Service Co. Ltd, which had a shipyard at Galmpton on the River Dart, to which the vessels returned each winter for a thorough overhaul, refit and repainting. This must have helped ensure the longevity of the craft. Two other Fairmile Bs survive in the UK: *Western Lady* (ex-RML 535) is laid up on the Dart in poor condition (she was the first of the RMLs to join the Western Lady Ferry service), and *Jamaican Moon* (ex-ML 357) is a houseboat at St Osyth.

Western Lady IV had originally been ordered for the Royal Navy on 27 August 1941 from Solent Shipyard Ltd, Lower Swanwick, on the River Hamble, and was completed as *RML 526* on 27 August 1942. She joined the 63rd ML Flotilla at Falmouth, and later transferred to the 61st ML Flotilla in the Portsmouth Command as an ambulance launch operating between Dover and Dartmouth.

Western Lady IV, in service as an excursion vessel, alongside at Brixham in 2003. (Steve Powell)

Western Lady IV in 2007 following her conversion to a yacht. (Owner)

For this work, she was based at Newhaven, until 1946, when she transferred to Plymouth. She was sold in March 1946, converted for use as a yacht and renamed *Anbrijo*. Between 1947 and 1949, she ran between Gibraltar and Tangier at a time when many ex-MLs were used in smuggling. She was arrested by the Admiralty Marshal in 1949 and subsequently sold at Fowey, becoming *Western Lady IV*, to operate between Brixham and Torquay – carrying up to 175 passengers. She was sold in 2007 to private owners Tony and Kim Medri and, in September of that year, sailed to Plymouth Sound to be berthed at Southdown Quay, Millbrook, Cornwall. A refit and restoration followed, in which the afterdeck saloon was removed, and she became a 'live-aboard' seagoing vessel. Her hull was repainted in dark blue.

Western Lady III had originally been ordered for the Royal Navy on 27 August 1941 from Southampton Steam Joinery Ltd, Southampton, and was completed as *RML 497* in July 1942. She served with the 62nd ML Flotilla at Portland until January 1944, when she was transferred to Kirkwall on anti-submarine target towing duties, and in August 1944, she was sent to Appledore. She then joined the 69th ML Flotilla at Felixstowe and was eventually sold at Itchenor in 1947. She entered service with the Western Lady Ferry Service, as *Western Lady III*, in that same year. In 2007, she was sold to Messrs Alastair Oliver and Colin Breach and, in July 2007, left Torbay for Poole to be operated from Swanage by Fairmile Classic Cruises. She only operated there for one season and by June 2009 had been impounded at Poole. She then was purchased by the Greenway Ferry Company, for service in south Devon and returned to Brixham on 26 June 2009. After a refit at Polruan, Cornwall, and renamed *The Fairmile*, the vessel started a service in July from Brixham and Torquay to Dartmouth and Greenway, the former home of murder mystery author Agatha Christie, which had been opened to the public by the National Trust for the first time in 2009.

Displacement: 85 tons (as ML). Gross tonnage (as passenger vessel): 108 (Western Lady III), 135 (Western Lady IV). Length: 112 feet (34.1 m). Beam: 18.25 feet (5.6 m). Draught: 4.6 feet (1.4 m).
Propulsion (as passenger vessels): twin Gardner 6LX diesels, 127 bhp each, twin screws. Speed: 10 knots cruising, 12 knots maximum.
Passengers: 175. Crew: 4.

HARBOUR DEFENCE MOTOR LAUNCHES

A large class of harbour defence motor launches (HDML) was built in the Second World War for anti-submarine patrol work in harbour, estuarial and inshore waters. The Admiralty design (by William Holt) was for a round chine 72-foot launch, and was kept simple so that they could be built by small boatyards at home and abroad. They proved sea-kindly craft and the success of the design led to them being used worldwide in a variety of roles in every theatre of operations. *ML 1387 (Medusa)* has survived to be restored to seagoing condition, after her

service as a survey launch had extended her Royal Navy career into the sixties.
Three other former HDMLs – *Morning Wings*, *Sarinda* and *Vincent* are also listed
on the National Historic Ships Register. Another five are listed by the *Medusa*
Trust as surviving in the UK: *Etive Shearwater* (ex-ML *1085*), *Marica* (ex-ML
1257) and *Abri* (ex-ML *1379*) as houseboats at Inverness, Hartlepool and Strood
respectively, whilst *Pride of the Dart* (ex-ML *1396*) at Torbay, and *TSR* (ex-ML
1422), sunk at her moorings at Birkenhead, are semi-derelict. In all, about thirty-
five former HDMLs are listed by the *Medusa* Trust as extant worldwide.

The HDML hull was constructed of double-diagonal mahogany planking (or larch
in some later vessels) on stringers with oak frames. The decks were double-diagonal
larch (or mahogany on some early vessels) and the superstructure was of marine ply.
They had two diesel engines and carried an armament of light anti-aircraft guns and
depth charges. The choice of guns was often dictated by availability, and variously
included 3, 2 and 1-pounders, 20-mm Oerlikons and 0.303-inch machine-guns.
494 boats were ordered, but thirty-two were cancelled and twenty were lost whilst
under construction due to bombing or the fall of Singapore.

The launches served in war theatres around the world. They rendered great
service during the evacuation of Crete, and acted as navigational leaders for
landing craft in Normandy, Sicily, Salerno and Arakan. They served as convoy
escorts off the north and west coasts of Africa. Some were fitted with minesweeping
equipment for use in sheltered waters.

ML 1387 was laid down by R. A. Newman at Hamworthy, Poole, on 27 July
1943, launched on 20 October and commissioned on 29 December of the same
year. On completion, she joined the HDML (Foreign Service) Pool at Poole, but
instead of serving overseas, she was involved in convoy escort in the Western
Approaches before joining the 149th HDML Flotilla at Portsmouth in Spring

Medusa as a survey motor launch in 1960. (World Ship Society)

The restored *ML 1387 (Medusa)* entering Portsmouth Harbour.

1944. She took part in Operation *Fabius I*, a practice assault carried out by the Americans at Slapton Sands in Devon. In June 1944, *ML 1387* was present at the D-Day landings, arriving off Omaha beach the night before and staying on station as a navigational marker for Approach Channel 4. In October 1944, she transferred to the 185th Auxiliary Minesweeping Flotilla based at Sheerness, to act as an escort to the flotilla. Early in 1945, she was at the Dutch coastal town of Ijmuiden, where she took the surrender of the occupying German forces. From Ijmuiden, she navigated the North Sea Canal to Amsterdam, the first Allied ship to do so.

In October 1945, she was refitted at Littlehampton and was renumbered *FDB 76* (fast despatch boat) and from February 1946 was attached to the Cardiff University Naval Division for training. Then, in February 1947, she was transferred to Severn Division RNVR for two years, providing seagoing training. In August 1949, renumbered *SDML 3516* (seaward defence motor launch), she was moved to London Division RNVR in the same capacity and then took the name *Thames*, the first in a line of vessels to take this name as a seagoing tender to that division. In November 1950, she was refitted and offered to the Persian government to replace another launch that had been damaged beyond repair en route to Persia, but the offer was refused.

In 1952, she was refitted at Chatham to become a survey motor launch, but kept the same number. Between 1952 and 1955, she was attached to the Survey Training Unit, Chatham. In 1956-57, the launch undertook independent surveys on the west coast of the UK, and, in 1958-60, was part of the East Coast Survey Unit. In March 1959, she was in collision with a Dutch coaster off Ramsgate in fog, and a three month refit followed. In March 1960, *SDML 3516* transferred to the Plymouth Command for surveys on the west and south coasts, between Torbay and the Solway Firth, and in 1961 was renamed *Medusa*. On 30 November 1965, she paid off for disposal at Devonport and whilst in reserve suffered fire damage.

Medusa was sold on 29 May 1968 to Mike Boyce, to be based at Portland as a motor yacht, still keeping her survey motor launch appearance. She was restored at Portland between 1972 and 1985, but remained seagoing for much of this time. In 1986, she was moved to Portsmouth Harbour to become a museum ship as part of an abortive plan by Gosport Borough Council to establish a Coastal Forces Museum. In 1997, she became the training tender to the Southampton Unit of the Maritime Volunteer Society. She is now under the care of the *Medusa* Trust and is operated in sea-going condition by volunteers from the *Medusa* Support Group. In 2006-09, *Medusa* was undergoing a major restoration and refit at Hythe Shipyard on Southampton Water, with the support of a £1 million grant from the Heritage Lottery Fund. The vessel was stripped down to bare frames, some of which were replaced. The hull was re-planked with triple teak, replacing double mahogany, and the vessel was re-decked. The engines, which date from 1940 and 1942 (having been fitted in a 1963 refit), were completely overhauled. However, in a fire at the shipyard on 30 October 2007, various valuable pieces of equipment and irreplaceable artefacts were lost and the engines were severely damaged, delaying completion of the work. The hull of *Medusa* was nearby in a temporary shelter and was not damaged. There are plans to exhibit her at Southampton as part of a proposed maritime heritage centre.

ML 1387
Displacement: 46 tons standard/54 tons full load. Length: 72 feet (21.9 m). Beam: 16 feet (4.87 m). Draught: 4.75 feet (1.4 m).
Propulsion: two Gardner diesel engines, 320 bhp, two shafts. Speed: 12 knots. Range: 2,000 miles at 10 knots. Bunkers: 1,650 gallons.
Armament: one 2-pounder and one 20-mm Oerlikon gun (later two 20-mm Oerlikon guns), twin 0.303-inch Vickers machine-guns, up to eight depth charges. (Now mounts two 20-mm Oerlikons).
Complement: 12 (two officers, two petty officers and eight ratings).
Pennant Numbers: ML 1387 (1943-45), FDB 76 (1945-49), P3516 (1949-61), A353 (1961-68).

Medusa's sister ship as a survey launch, *Meda* (formerly *ML 1301*), latterly named *Gibel Tarik* in private ownership, is at Ijmuiden, Holland, undergoing restoration to something close to her original appearance.

Morning Wings was built as *ML 1309* by G. Bunn, Wroxham, and completed on 4 February 1944. As part of the 149th ML Flotilla, she was a navigation leader

Marica, formerly *ML 1257*, as a houseboat at Hartlepool, in August 2007. (Author)

Sarinda as a luxury motor yacht. (Owner)

for the D-Day landings in June 1944. After the war, she continued in service as the fast despatch boat *FDB 75*. She was sold by the Admiralty on 14 April 1948 and was used for smuggling at Gibraltar in the 1950s and 1960s until being caught and impounded. She then became a houseboat until 1989, when her present owner purchased her and motored her back to the UK from Gibraltar (she still has her original twin 160-bhp Gleniffer diesels). *Morning Wings* is now at Upton upon Severn, Worcestershire undergoing restoration.

Sarinda was built as *ML 1392* by Berthon Boats, Lymington, and completed on 20 December 1943. Also part of the 149th ML Flotilla, she was a navigation leader at Gold Beach during the D-Day landings in June 1944. On 6 March 1945, she captured a Biber-type German midget submarine off Breskens in the Scheldt estuary. After the war, she continued in service as the fast despatch boat *FDB 73*. In October 1947, she was transferred to HM Customs & Excise and renamed *Valiant*. In about 1967, she was sold and became the motor yacht *Frol-Pejo*. By 1974, she had been renamed *Sarinda*. A total rebuild as a luxury motor yacht was started in 1979 and completed by a new owner after she was sold on 1987. She is now based at Liverpool.

Vincent was built as *ML 1300* by M. W. Blackmore & Sons Ltd, Bideford, and completed on 20 January 1943. Her war service included protection of the Weymouth anchorage during the build up to the Normandy invasion. After the war, she continued in service as the fast despatch boat *FDB 64*. In June 1948, she was transferred to HM Customs & Excise and renamed *Vincent*. In 1969, she was sold to John Hudson of Cardiff and had a new aluminium deckhouse added. She

Morning Wings undergoing restoration at Upton upon Severn. (Neil Farthing)

One of the Gleniffer diesel engines in *Morning Wings*. (Neil Farthing)

was refitted and operated out of Cardiff and Brixham, before being sold to the Lomer Seamanship & Navigation Centre in 1976 for use as their training flagship in the Solent area. *Vincent* is now under private ownership as a motor yacht based at Carrickfergus, Northern Ireland.

HSL 102 – AIR SEA RESCUE LAUNCH

The Royal Navy's first motor torpedo boats were ordered in 1935 by the Admiralty from the British Power Boat Co. (BPB) at Hythe, on Southampton Water. They were 60 feet in length and a stretched version of their hard chine planing hull was used for twenty-two air sea rescue launches of the 100 class ordered for the Royal Air Force from BPB. The RAF's Air Sea Rescue Service, in which these boats served, was to be credited with saving 10,000 airmen's lives in the Second World War – from 'ditched' aircraft, both Allied and German. In such work, speed was of the essence, since the airmen in the sea were vulnerable to hypothermia and were often wounded.

HSL 102, the only survivor of the 100 class, was launched in 1936 and entered service in the following year. Of mahogany double-diagonal construction, she was powered by three Napier Sea Lion petrol engines. During the Battle of Britain, she was mostly based at Blyth, Northumberland. Her war service also included periods

HSL 102 at Portsmouth's International Festival of the Sea in 1998. (Author)

based on the Firth of Forth and at Calshot. In two months in 1941, she rescued thirty-eight aircrew from the North Sea, including the crews of two German bombers. As a result, she was inspected by King George VI and Queen Elizabeth in July 1941. When working off Calshot, she was damaged by a Messerschmitt 109 and her radio operator was killed. In 1943, she was transferred to the Royal Navy for target towing, and paid off in 1946.

She became a houseboat in Mill Creek at Dartmouth and was in a sorry state when acquired by Phil Clabburn for restoration. The extensive work needed was carried out by Powerboat Restorations at Fawley between 1993 and 1996. Three six-cylinder 420-bhp Cummins diesels were installed, giving a top speed of about 38 knots. On 5 July 1996, *HSL 102* was relaunched at Fawley by Queen Elizabeth the Queen Mother, and was subsequently based at Lymington, Hampshire. In late 2009 she moved to Portsmouth following her acquisition by the Portsmouth Naval Base Property Trust, with the help of a grant from the National Heritage Memorial Fund.

Displacement: 46.6 tons. Length: 71.5 feet. (21.8 m). Beam: 20.5 feet. (6.25 m). Draught: 5.75 feet. (1.75 m).
Propulsion (as built): three 500-bhp Napier Sea Lion petrol engines, three shafts. Speed: 40 knots.
Fuel bunkers: 950 gallons (4,300 l).

RTTL 2757 – RESCUE AND TARGET TOWING LAUNCH

Also referred to as HMAFV 2757, or RAF Marine Craft 2757, this rescue and target towing launch (RTTL) was one of a class of fifteen 68-foot-high speed launches and was launched in 1957 by Vosper Ltd, Portsmouth, for the Royal Air Force. She was powered by Rolls-Royce Sea-Griffon high-octane petrol engines, a marine version of the Griffon range of aero-engines. Her hull was of double-diagonal mahogany planking, and the superstructure was of aluminium. Her principal role was target towing for RAF strike and anti-submarine aircraft, but RTTLs were also equipped for search and rescue operations, including the rescue of downed aircrews. The RAF operated a large fleet of differing marine craft at coastal stations worldwide until the 1980s. The 68-foot launches were the only craft entitled to use the HMAFV (Her Majesty's Air Force Vessel) designation.

RTTL 2757 was delivered new to RAF Alness in January 1958 and, on 23 January, was allocated to 1100 Marine Craft Unit there. In August 1965, she moved to RAF Mountbatten, Plymouth, for repairs. In June 1966, she joined 1105 Marine Craft Unit at Portrush, Northern Ireland and stayed there until 4 February 1971 when the unit was closed and she moved to RAF Mountbatten, Plymouth. In 1974-75, the vessel completed some fifty operational exercises/sorties, mainly involving RAF aircraft, though with some work with the Royal Navy and the army. She became the last of her class in service and was kept maintained at Mountbatten until being gifted to the RAF Museum, Hendon, on 22 November 1977. On 26 November, she left Plymouth and arrived at London's Royal Victoria Docks two days later. She was moved by road to Hendon on 4 December to become a permanent exhibit on the edge of the car park.

Displacement: 34 tons. Length: 68 feet (20.73 m). Beam: 19 feet (5.8 m). Draught: 5.9 feet (1.8 m).
Propulsion: Two twelve-cylinder Rolls-Royce Sea-Griffon high-octane petrol engines, each of 1,450 bhp, twin screws. Speed: 39 knots.
Crew: 9. Passengers: 120 max.

MFVs – NAVAL TENDERS

The wartime requirement for tenders to service the expanded number of naval ports and anchorages led to the adoption of commercial motor fishing vessel (MFV) designs by the Admiralty during the Second World War, and around 850 were built. They were used for ferrying personnel and stores in harbours and inshore waters, both at home and abroad, and some of the largest type were fitted as minesweepers. A light gun was usually mounted (either 0.303 inches or 20 mm). They were flush-decked, wooden-hulled with a round bilge, had a single hold forward, and were built by small boatyards in the UK, South Africa and Australia.

RTTL 2757 at speed during her service days. (RAF Museum)

Although many were sold for commercial use when the war ended, the four types all survived in large numbers in postwar Admiralty service. In 1963, for example, there were fifty-five boats of the 65-foot type, twenty-five boats of the 50-foot type, thirty-six of the 75-foot type, and five of the 97-foot type in Port Auxiliary Service, and a number were serving with the army. Some of these were still in naval service in the mid-seventies.

Survivors (now in private ownership) listed in the National Register of Historic Vessels in 2009 were as follows.

65-FOOT TYPE

MFV 74

Built in 1946 by Curtis & Pape, Looe, Cornwall, and worked for the Admiralty at Plymouth until 1974, when she was sold to a private owner. She later became derelict at Milford Haven and was resold in 2002 for restoration to full operating condition, still based at Milford Haven under the original name, *MFV 74*.

MFV 119

Built by J. Morris, Gosport, and completed in February 1944. She went to Omaha beach with an American crew in the D-Day landings of June 1944 and was later

MFV 74. (A. McCloud)

MFV 119 leaving Portsmouth in 1985. (Michael Lennon)

used as a dive boat on the wreck of the *Mary Rose* in the early stages of research. She was based at Rosyth in 1963. Now at Cowes, Isle of Wight, undergoing conversion to a fully operational motor yacht, and retains the original name *MFV 119*.

MFV 175 – Dream Trader

Built by F. Curtis, Looe, and completed in October 1945. She was reportedly sold in 1955 and became *St Cecilia*, but returned to Admiralty service in the same year. She was based on the Clyde in 1963, and was renamed *Sultan Venturer* in later years, presumably as a tender to HMS *Sultan*, Gosport. She was sold in 1988 for use as a leisure craft, renamed *Dream Trader*, and is now based at Falmouth.

Displacement: 50 tons. Length: 64.5 feet (19.66 m). Beam: 17.75 feet (5.4 m). Draught: 10 feet (3 m).
Propulsion: Kelvin diesel engine, 88 bhp, (some craft had other makers' diesels), single screw.
Speed: 8.5 knots. Range: 100 nm at 9 knots. Bunkers: 450 gallons.
Complement: 6.

50-FOOT TYPE

MFV 613 – Cornish Maiden

Ordered from James Martin & Sons, Midlothian, in December 1942, and completed in May 1944 for the Admiralty. She worked at Portsmouth until being sold in February 1948 to Trinity House. Renamed *Burhou*, she was then used as a pilot/work boat in the Channel Islands, supplying the Casquet lighthouse. She became one of Trinity House's longest serving vessels until being sold in 1989. Now named *Cornish Maiden*, she is based at Erith, Kent.

Cornish Maiden. (Neil Meekums)

MFV 740

Completed in March 1945 by J. Bolson, Poole. Her early service was on the Thames and at Lowestoft until December 1945. She then moved to Rosyth to service the reserve fleet there until early 1950, when she moved to the Clyde for further Admiralty service. In 1953, a new Foden engine was installed. In November 1981, she was transferred to the Northern area Sea Cadet Corps. In 1987, she was sold to her present owner for leisure use. She is now based at Prenton, Wirral, and retains the original name *MFV 740*.

MFV 797 – Old 797

Completed in November 1945 by Wallasea Bay Yacht Station Ltd, Wallesey. She was sold in 1945 (or 1969, sources differ) and reconditioned between 1969 and 1974 to become the motor yacht *Old 797*, based at Annan, Scotland. She cruised and chartered off the west coast of Scotland and ventured as far afield as St Kilda and Norway. Later, she was sold to the sea scouts. Resold, she is now at Runnymede, on the Thames, where her current owner, Mark Humphrey, is refitting her afloat. Her current engine is a Perkins diesel.

Displacement: 28.5 tons. Length: 49.75 feet (15.2 m). Beam: 16.25 feet (5 m). Draught: 8.5 feet (2.6 m).
Propulsion: Atlantic or Chrysler petrol engine, 60 bhp, single screw. Could be rigged with sails when sailing to an overseas station.
Speed: 7.5 knots. Range: 300 nm at 7.5 knots. Bunkers: 142 gallons.
Complement: 4.

97-FOOT TYPE

MFV 1502 – Navigator

Completed on 30 December 1943 by Richards Ironworks Co. Ltd, Lowestoft, who also designed this class. She was commissioned on 5 January 1944 and allocated to Force S at Inverness on 8 January. She was then sent to Great Yarmouth for tropicalisation but was required to escort a convoy with *MFV 1503*. She was then reportedly present at the D-Day landings. On completion of these duties, she was at Portsmouth on 21 July 1944 for a short refit. In March 1945, she was sent to Wivenhoe Shipyard to complete the tropicalisation and conversion to a fireboat. *MFV 1502* was army manned from May 1945 and operated around the South Coast for the remainder of the year. In 1947, she was transferred permanently to the army and manned by a Royal Army Service Corps (RASC) crew. She was attached to the Water Transport Company 985 and used for navigational training, with a grey livery, and was listed under the name MV 1502. In the late fifties, she was modernised with an enlarged bridge, and a forward deckhouse was added, and, in 1959, she became civilian-manned. By the seventies, a second modernisation had given her a streamlined funnel, stump mast and deckhouse extended further forward, and had a navy blue hull, white upperworks and buff funnel. By 1962, she had been renamed *Yarmouth Navigator* and, in 1965, became part of the Royal Corps of Transport, following the merger of the RASC with the Royal Engineers. By 1976, the vessel was attached to the Fleet Squadron 20 Maritime Regiment, Royal Corps of Transport, based at Gunwharf, Portsmouth. Later, she was with 18 Maritime Squadron, still used for navigational training as well as range duties. On 1 October 1988, she was transferred with other army vessels to the RMAS (Royal

Navigator. (National Historic Ships)

MFV 1502 seen at Portsmouth in 1956. (World Ship Society)

Maritime Auxiliary Service) under Royal Navy control: *Yarmouth Navigator* led a sail past at a final Army Fleet Review at Spithead on 30 September 1988. In April 1990, she became a training tender for the Sea Cadet Corps at Portsmouth and was briefly listed as *Yarmouth Voyager.* She was then the oldest seagoing vessel in MOD service. In October 1990, she was laid up at Portsmouth, and was sold in 1991 as *Yarmouth Navigator* to Lt Cdr J. McGuire of Dartmouth and sailed to the River Dart. She has since been sold and, now named *Navigator,* is reported to be undergoing a restoration programme at Dartmouth.

Displacement: 200 tons. Length: 97.25 feet (29.6 m). Beam: 22.25 feet (6.9 m). Draught: 12.25 feet (3.7 m).
Propulsion: Crossley four-cylinder diesel engine, 240 bhp, single shaft.
Speed: 9.25 knots. Range: 2,160 nm at 9 knots. Bunkers: 23 tons oil fuel.
Complement: 11. Cargo capacity: 35 tons.

Index of Ship Names

Abri, 146
Advance, 92, 94
Alaska, 53-54
Balmoral, 44-47
Barcadale, 116-17
Basuto, 87-88
Bertha, 108-109
Blue Linnet, 116-18
Brent, 75
Brocklebank, 76-77
Bronington, 126-31
C668, 98
Calshot, 76-77
Canning, 61-62
Carola, 122-23
Cervia, 61-62
Challenge, 63-65
Compton Castle, 17-19
Cornish Maiden, 156-57
Coronia, 54-55
Cuddington, 88-89
Daniel Adamson, 65-66
Destiny, 85
Dream Trader, 156
Edmund Gardner, 108, 110
Egremont, 47-48
Esperance, 123-24
Etive Shearwater, 146
Explorer, 111-12
Freshspring, 99-100
Garnock, 79-80
Gondola, 30-33
HSL 102, 151-52
Hurlingham, 56-57
Iveston, 126, 131-32
James Jackson Grundy, 89-90
John Adams, 112
John H. Amos, 67-68
John King, 80-81
Karina, 57-58
Kenilworth, 58-59
Kent, 81-82
Kerne, 68-69
Kingswear Castle, 15-17
Knocker White, 82-83
Kyles, 101-102
Lady of the Lake, 37-39
Lady Wakefield, 40-41
Lincoln Castle, 19, 24
Lydia Eva, 118-120
Maggie, 94-96
Maid of the Loch, 28-29
Manxman, 49-50
Marica, 146, 149
Mayflower, 70-71
Medusa, 145-48
Medway Queen, 24-27

ML 1387, 145-48
MFV 74, 155
MFV 119, 155-56
MFV 175, 156
MFV 613, 156
MFV 740, 157
MFV 797, 157
MFV 1502, 158-59
MGB 81, 139-41
Morning Wings, 148-51
MTB 71, 138-39
MTB 102, 134-38
MTB 416, 140-41
Navigator, 158-59
Nomadic, 50-52
Northern Belle, 59-60
Old 797, 157
Portwey, 71-73
Pyronaut, 113-14
Raven, 39-40
Raven, 102-103
Regal Lady, 55-56
RML 511, 142
Robin, 103-106
Ross Leopard, 120-21
Ross Tiger, 120-21
RTTL 2757, 153-54
Safe Hand, 90-91
Sarinda, 149-50
Severn Progress, 82-84
Shieldhall, 106-107
Sir Walter Scott, 42-43
Spartan, 93, 95
Swan, 35-37
Tattershall Castle, 19-24
Teal, 35-37
Tern, 33-35
The Fairmile, 145
Thomas, 84-85
TID 164, 73-75
TID 172, 73-75
Ton class, 126-34
Undine, 125
VIC 32, 92, 94-95
VIC 56, 96-99
VIC 96, 96-99
Vigilant, 114-15
Vincent, 150-51
Vital Spark, 93, 95
Waverley, 11-15
Wendy Ann, 84, 86
Western Lady III, 143-45
Western Lady IV, 142-45
Wilton, 126, 132-34
Wingfield Castle, 19-20, 22-23
Yarmouth Belle, 60